MISA YA MT. SESILIA
NA NYIMBO ZA LITURUJIA

(St. Cecilia Mass and Other Liturgical Songs)

Wilson Shitandi

Songburd Music, LLC
www.songburdmusic.com

Cover art: *Saint Cecilia* by Giovanni Francesco Barbieri (1649)

St. Cecilia Mass and other Liturgical Songs
Words and music by Wilson Shitandi
Copyright © 2025 Wilson Shitandi
All rights reserved. International copyright secure.

Printed and distributed by Songburd Music

Print ISBN: 978-1-952680-28-1
Digital ISBN: 978-1-952680-29-8

MISA YA MT. SESILIA
SAINT CECILIA MASS

Entrance Hymns
Mwimbieni Bwana — 1
Tujongee Nyumba ya Bwana — 10

Penitential Rites
Bwana 'tuhurumie (*Kyrie Eleison*) — 21
Utukufu (*Gloria*) — 26

The Liturgy of the Word
Yawa Uling'aling'a (*Gospel Procession*) — 36
Kumbuka Rehema Zako (*Psalm*) — 46
Alleluia (*Gospel Acclamation*) — 60

The Creed
Nasadiki (*Credo*) — 61

The Prayer of the Faithful
Nzambe Tata — 71

Offertory
Ewe Mungu Baba Bariki (*Offertory Collection*) — 74
Mungu Tunaleta Sadaka (*Offertory Procession*) — 85

The Liturgy of the Eucharist
Mtakatifu (*Sanctus*) — 92
Kristu Alikufa Kristu Alifufuka (*Proclamation of Our Faith*) — 97
Pamoja Naye (*Lesser Doxology*) — 99
Amina (*Amen*) — 100

The Communion Rites
Baba Yetu (*Pater Nostre*) — 101
Amani ya Bwana (*The Sign of Peace*) — 111
Ee Mwna Kondoo (*Agnus Dei*) — 121

Holy Communion
Posho la Mbingu — 125
Kusali Kweli ni Heria — 142

Thanksgiving
Nakutegemea Mwenyezi — 151

Recessional Hymns
Unirehemu Unitakase — 170

PREFACE

St. Cecilia Mass: Origin and Purpose

The conception of St. Cecilia Mass emerged from a dual necessity—academic and liturgical. While pursuing my graduate studies at Kenyatta University, I was required to complete a compositional project as part of my academic program. Concurrently, as Director of the St. Cecilia Holy Cross Choir at Dandora Parish, Nairobi, I was tasked by the choir leadership to compose a Mass dedicated to the choir, one that would serve as its official liturgical setting. This convergence of academic obligation and pastoral responsibility gave birth to St. Cecilia Mass. Since its completion in 2005, the Mass has transcended its initial context, becoming a staple not only within Dandora Holy Cross Parish but also in numerous parishes across Nairobi and other regions of Kenya.

Style, Thematic, and Structural Ideas

St. Cecilia Holy Cross Choir is situated in a cosmopolitan environment, comprising singers from diverse Kenyan ethnic communities. Kenya boasts approximately fifty-two distinct ethnic groups, each with unique musical idioms, and many of these are represented within the choir. One of the greatest challenges in crafting St. Cecilia Mass was determining how to incorporate these varied musical styles into a unified liturgical work. My primary goal as composer and director was to ensure that members of these communities could identify with the Mass by recognizing idioms resonant with their cultural heritage.

The five principal sections of the Ordinary of the Mass—Kyrie (Bwana Utuhurumie), Gloria (Utukufu), Credo (Nasadiki), Sanctus (Mtakatifu), and Agnus Dei (Mwana Kondoo)—formed the structural foundation. To address the challenge of representing multiple traditions, I extended the work to include additional hymns from the Proper of the Mass, such as the Introit, Gradual (Responsorial Psalm), Alleluia (Gospel Acclamation), Pater Noster (Our Father), Communion, and Offertory hymns. Thus, the term St. Cecilia Mass in these notes refers not only to the five Ordinary parts but to the complete liturgical repertoire associated with the celebration.

The Mass integrates original compositional ideas, arranged themes, and adapted popular tunes. Original ideas primarily manifest in pitch configurations and structural frameworks, often grounded in rhythmic patterns inspired by traditional idioms of the communities represented. For instance, those familiar with Luhya musical traditions will recognize their influence in Utukufu, while Kamba idioms appear in Baba Yetu and Mwana Kondoo. Luo stylistic elements permeate the Gospel Procession hymn, and contemporary popular styles are evident in Nasadiki and Mtakatifu.

Melodic ideas are predominantly diatonic and cyclic, characterized by repetition and a call-and-response structure. This deliberate choice reflects both African musical aesthetics and the directives of Vatican II, particularly the Sacrosanctum Concilium and Musicam Sacram, which encourage composers to foster active participation and incorporate indigenous musical forms, provided they align with the general characteristics of sacred music.

Philosophical Significance of Repetition Elements in the Mass

The cyclic, call-and-response structure employed in St. Cecilia Mass draws inspiration from African musical traditions, where a soloist introduces a melodic phrase and the chorus responds, creating an endlessly repeatable cycle. This repetition is not merely a structural device

but a profound cultural and philosophical element that serves multiple functions:
Community and Participation: Repetition fosters collective music-making, reinforcing social harmony and interdependence.

Spiritual Transcendence and Healing: Sustained rhythmic repetition can induce meditative states, facilitating spiritual connection and renewal.
Communication and Storytelling: Repetition aids in preserving oral traditions, reinforcing memory, and transmitting cultural values.
Aesthetic Complexity: Ostinato patterns provide a stable framework for intricate polyrhythms, inviting active, creative listening.

Resilience and Endurance: In Black musical aesthetics, repetition asserts strength and continuity, even in adversity. Thus, repetition in African music is a deliberate philosophical choice, enabling profound social, spiritual, and aesthetic functions.

Theological Foundations of Repetition Structures in the Mass
The repetitive nature of the Mass is also rooted in theological principles. In worship, repetition serves to deepen meditation, emphasize divine truths, and bridge the gap between intellectual understanding and spiritual transformation. Biblical precedent abounds: Psalm 136 repeats "His steadfast love endures forever" twenty-six times, while Revelation 4:8 depicts eternal praise through the ceaseless repetition of "Holy, holy, holy is the Lord God Almighty." Such patterns underscore the role of repetition in fostering contemplation and spiritual formation.

Theological Rationale for Repetition
Beyond biblical precedent, repetition serves as a tool for meditation and reflection. It allows divine truths to penetrate the heart, moving from mere intellectual comprehension to deep spiritual understanding. Like chewing the cud, repetition enables worshipers to draw out the full nourishment of God's Word. Theologically, repetition emphasizes truth. The Apostle Paul demonstrates this in Philippians 4:4: "Rejoice in the Lord always; again I say, rejoice!" Such reiteration cements the message in the minds of believers. Over time, repeated phrases in liturgy and song shape spiritual formation, transforming belief from analysis into instinct and forming Christian reflexes that guide daily living. Repetition also fosters unity in corporate worship. Singing the same words allows diverse congregations to unite in one voice, focusing their collective attention on God. It aids memory, making participation accessible to all. Furthermore, music combined with repetition creates an emotional bridge, giving worshipers space for their hearts to align with the truths they sing.

In my experience, congregants often recall and hum recurring musical themes long after the service—while cooking, working, walking, or even shopping. These melodies become companions in daily life, reinforcing faith beyond the sanctuary. Remarkably, some themes transcend denominational boundaries, promoting musical ecumenism. Rarely do I hear worshipers recall through-composed works with the same enthusiasm. Repetition, therefore, is not mere musical technique; it is a profound theological and pastoral tool.

Notes on Performance Directions

The *St. Cecilia Mass* integrates African traditional and contemporary musical idioms, characterized by rhythmic vitality and interwoven syncopated layers that naturally invite movement and percussion. Directors and singers are encouraged to exercise creative freedom in selecting instruments and bodily expressions, provided these enhance rather than hinder the liturgical flow. Traditional African drums such as the djembe may be used to enrich texture and deepen cultural resonance. Additionally, it is also recognized that certain pieces set in F major may feel low for some choirs. Directors are therefore advised to exercise discretion in transposing these works by a semitone or whole tone upward, for example to F-Sharp major or G major, ensuring a tonality that is comfortable for both the singers and the congregation. Ultimately, the guiding principle is to balance musical integrity with accessibility and participation.

Dynamic markings in the score are intended as guides rather than rigid prescriptions. Choirs may interpret dynamics according to their context and artistic imagination, ensuring effective delivery and authentic expression.

Liturgical Imperatives

This Mass is composed with the Roman Catholic Eucharistic celebration in mind. Choirs should strive to maintain the order of the Mass and avoid interspersing its principal parts with unrelated hymns or excerpts from other settings. Each section is crafted to convey specific meaning and mood appropriate to its place in the celebration. Deliberate interrelatedness and structural interdependence of various components were key factors in the compositional thought processes of the Mass.

It is important to note that the Responsorial Psalm included here may not correspond to the readings of a given day. Choristers should consult parish liturgists to ensure alignment with the liturgical calendar. Similarly, introits and recessional hymns should reflect the themes of the day's readings.

While designed for Catholic worship, many hymns in this collection can serve other Christian communities. The texts draw primarily from Scripture and common liturgical prayers, making this work a resource for edification and spiritual formation across traditions.

Acknowledgment

The realization of this publication would not have been possible without the dedication and professionalism of Sean Burdette and the entire team at Songburd Music Publishing. Their expertise and attention to detail have produced a work of exceptional quality that will serve musicians and worshipers alike.
I am deeply grateful to my academic mentors, fellow directors, colleagues, friends, family, and the leadership and members of St. Cecilia Holy Cross Choir. Your commitment—whether through rehearsals, recordings, or countless acts of service—has been invaluable. Special thanks to the choir for producing the audio recording featured in their first volume. May the Lord bless and keep you always.

Above all, I thank Almighty God for His grace and the gifts of music, voice, leadership, and teaching. May He continue to use me as an instrument of evangelization through the art of music.

Dedication

This work is lovingly dedicated to the St. Cecilia Holy Cross Choir of Dandora Parish. During my tenure as your director, I witnessed your unwavering faith and resilience. In the face of adversity and economic hardship, you poured yourselves into practice, animated liturgies, cared for the sick, buried the dead, welcomed new life, and mounted concerts with joy and hope. Your spirit of brotherhood and selfless service remains unmatched. You are true pilgrims of faith and hope.

First Edition: Inviting Your Feedback

As this is our first edition, we recognize that it may include errors, omissions, unnecessary details, or unintended misrepresentations. We sincerely apologize for any confusion these may cause and appreciate your understanding. Your feedback is invaluable in helping us improve future editions. We warmly welcome your suggestions, corrections, and recommendations to make this work more accurate, insightful, and enriching. Words of encouragement are also greatly appreciated—they inspire us to keep striving for excellence.

Please share your thoughts via email at **shitandiw@gmail.com** or **contact@songburdmusic.com**. Your input will play a vital role in shaping a stronger second edition.

Thank you for your support and engagement!

"And to God be the Glory"

Mwimbieni Bwana

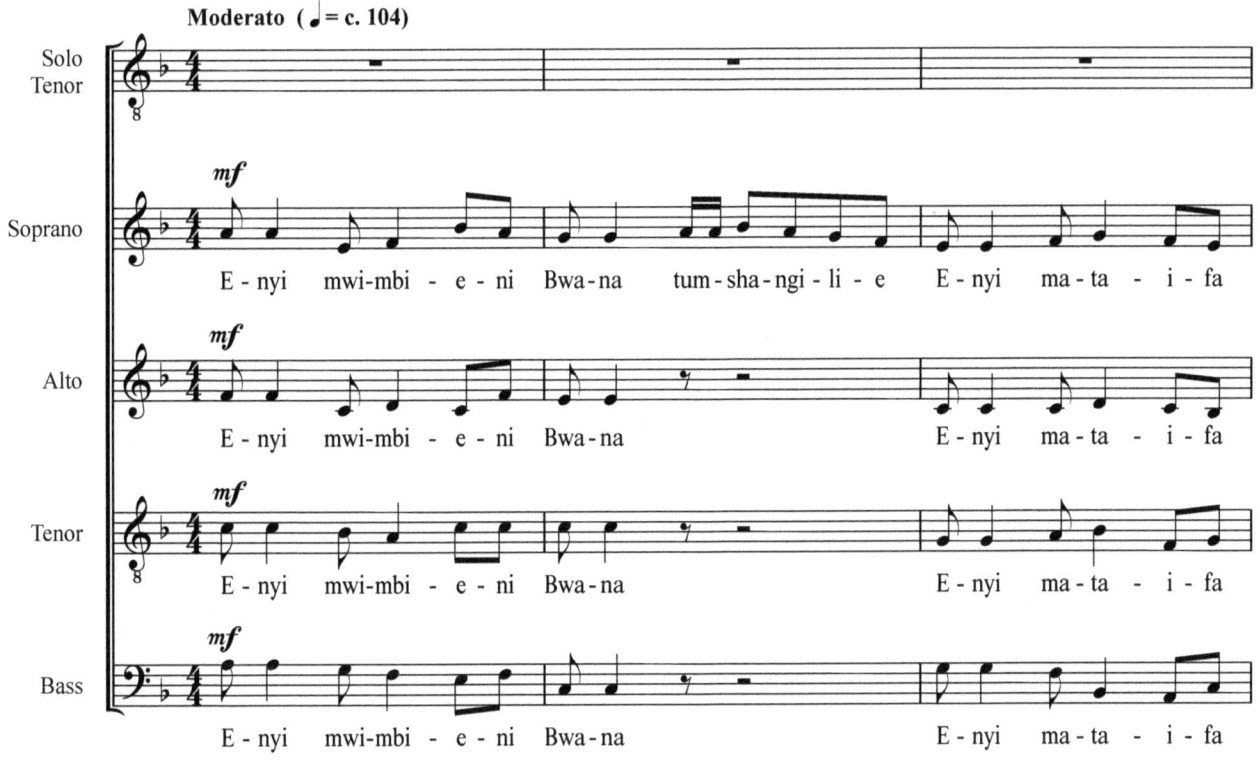

Mwimbieni Bwana

Mwimbieni Bwana

Mwimbieni Bwana

Mwimbieni Bwana

Mwimbieni Bwana

Mwimbieni Bwana

Tujongee Nyumba ya Bwana

Tujongee Nyumba ya Bwana

Tujongee Nyumba ya Bwana

14   Tujongee Nyumba ya Bwana

Tujongee Nyumba ya Bwana

Tujongee Nyumba ya Bwana

Tujongee Nyumba ya Bwana

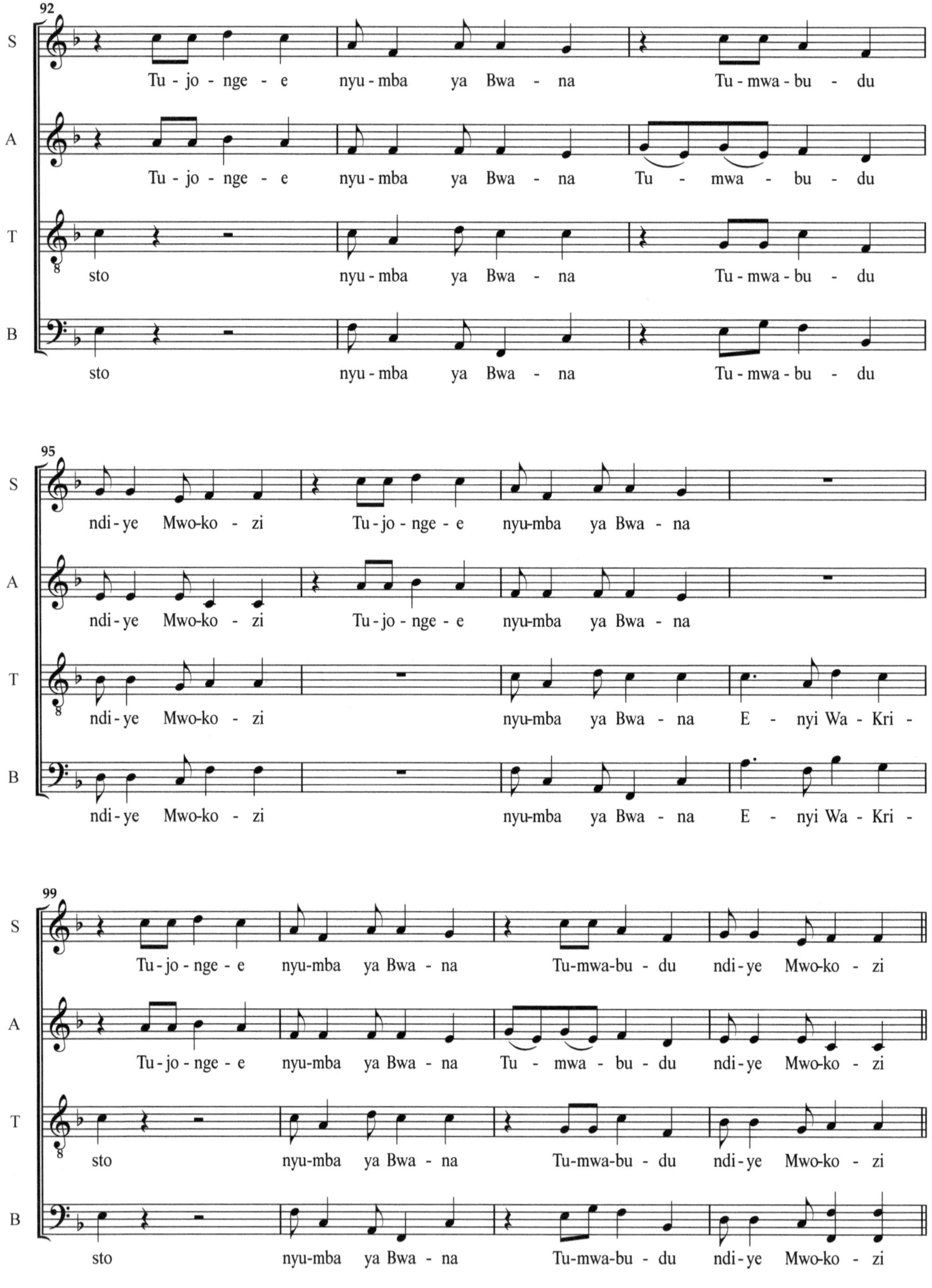
92
S
Tu - jo - nge - e nyu - mba ya Bwa - na Tu - mwa - bu - du
A
Tu - jo - nge - e nyu - mba ya Bwa - na Tu - mwa - bu - du
T
sto nyu - mba ya Bwa - na Tu - mwa - bu - du
B
sto nyu - mba ya Bwa - na Tu - mwa - bu - du
95
S
ndi - ye Mwo-ko - zi Tu - jo - nge - e nyu-mba ya Bwa - na
A
ndi - ye Mwo-ko - zi Tu - jo - nge - e nyu-mba ya Bwa - na
T
ndi - ye Mwo-ko - zi nyu-mba ya Bwa - na E - nyi Wa - Kri -
B
ndi - ye Mwo-ko - zi nyu-mba ya Bwa - na E - nyi Wa - Kri -
99
S
Tu - jo - nge - e nyu-mba ya Bwa - na Tu-mwa-bu - du ndi - ye Mwo-ko - zi
A
Tu - jo - nge - e nyu-mba ya Bwa - na Tu - mwa - bu - du ndi - ye Mwo-ko - zi
T
sto nyu-mba ya Bwa - na Tu-mwa-bu - du ndi - ye Mwo-ko - zi
B
sto nyu-mba ya Bwa - na Tu-mwa-bu - du ndi - ye Mwo-ko - zi

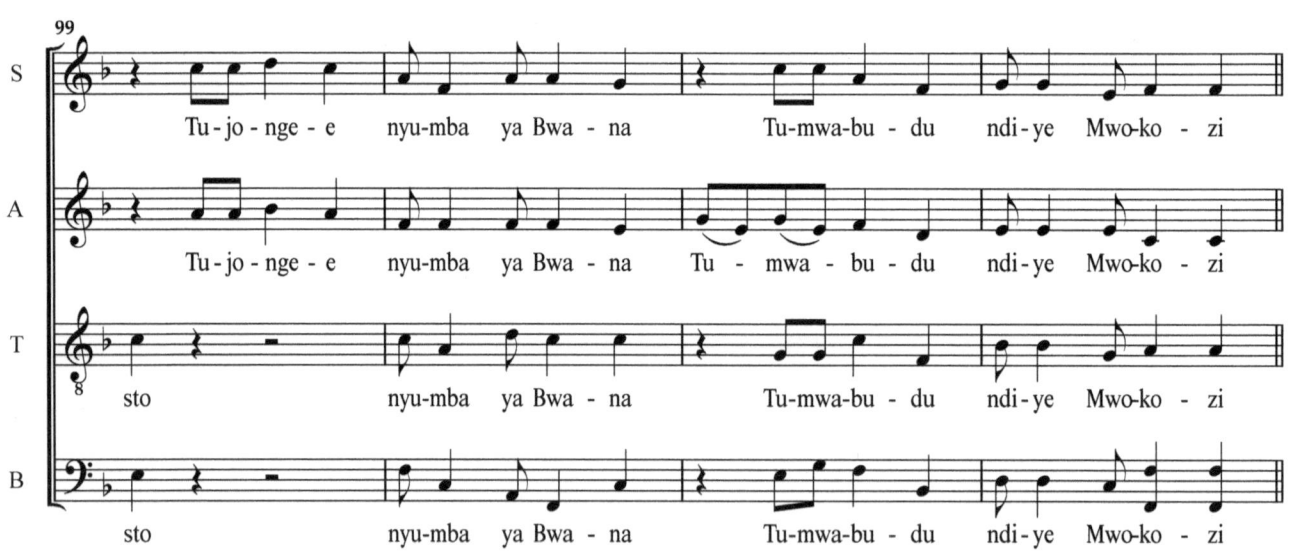

Bwana 'tuhurumie
Kyrie Eleison

Bwana 'tuhurumie

Bwana 'tuhurumie

Bwana 'tuhurumie

Utukufu
Gloria

Utukufu

Utukufu

Utukufu

Utukufu

Utukufu

Yawa Uling'aling'a
Gospel Procession

Kumbuka Rehema Zako
Psalm

Kumbuka Rehema Zako

Kumbuka Rehema Zako

Kumbuka Rehema Zako

Kumbuka Rehema Zako

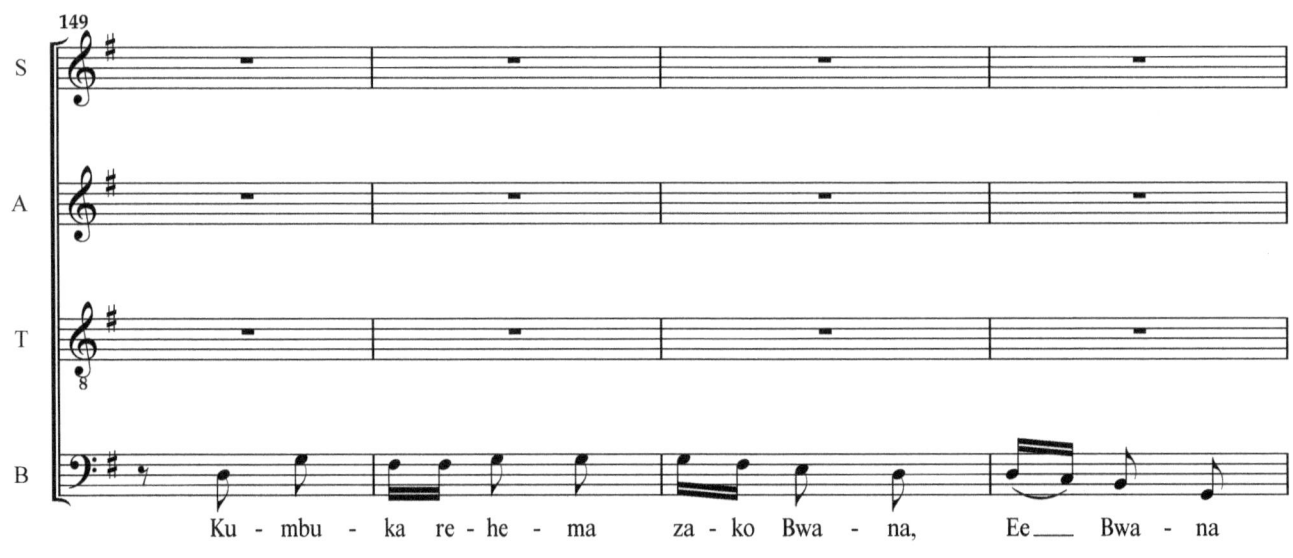

Alleluia
Gospel Acclamation

Nasadiki
Credo

Nasadiki

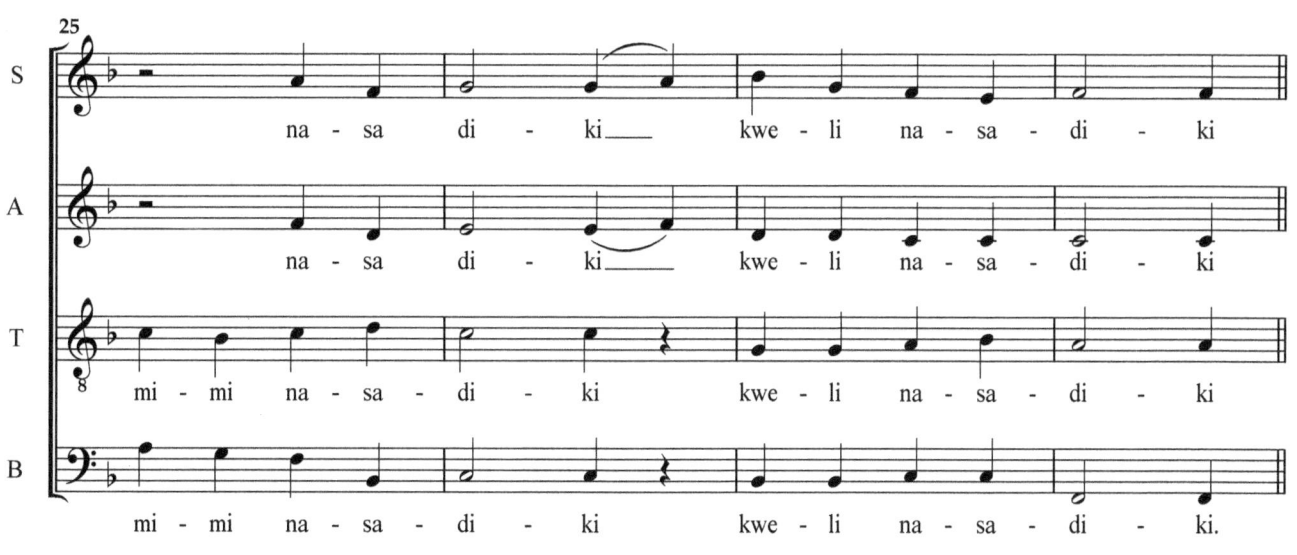

Nasadiki

Nasadiki

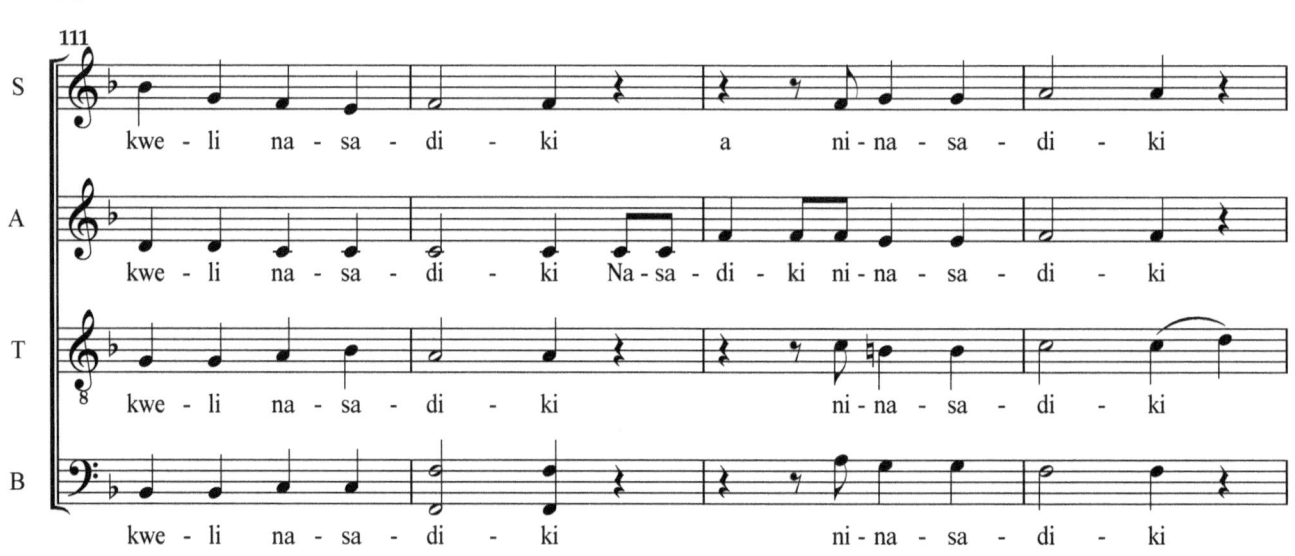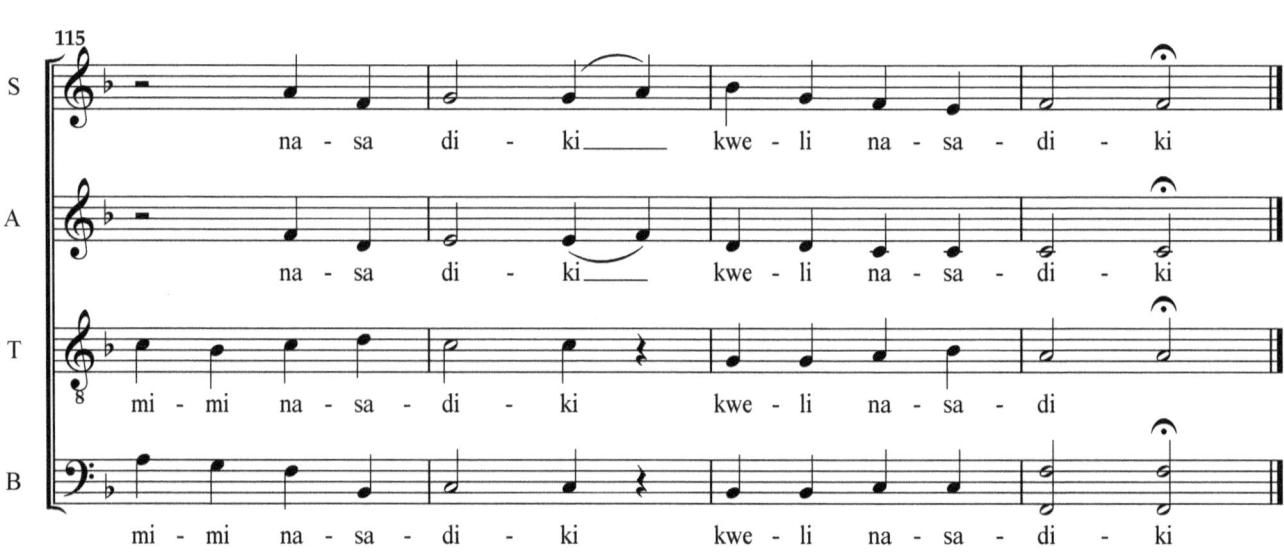

Nzambe Tata

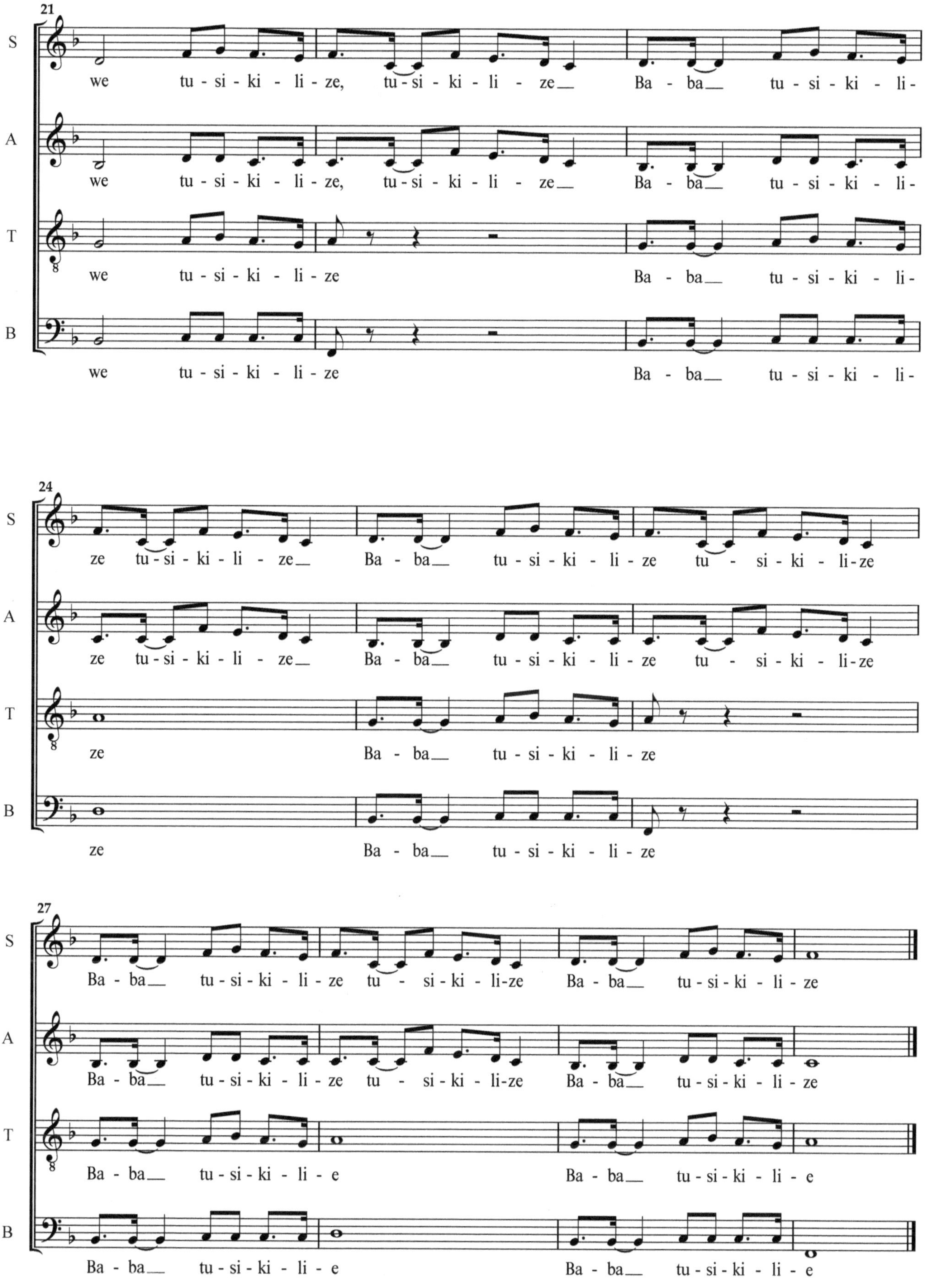
21
S
we tu - si - ki - li - ze, tu - si - ki - li - ze Ba - ba tu - si - ki - li-
A
we tu - si - ki - li - ze, tu - si - ki - li - ze Ba - ba tu - si - ki - li-
T
we tu - si - ki - li - ze Ba - ba tu - si - ki - li-
B
we tu - si - ki - li - ze Ba - ba tu - si - ki - li-
24
S
ze tu - si - ki - li - ze Ba - ba tu - si - ki - li - ze tu - si - ki - li - ze
A
ze tu - si - ki - li - ze Ba - ba tu - si - ki - li - ze tu - si - ki - li - ze
T
ze Ba - ba tu - si - ki - li - ze
B
ze Ba - ba tu - si - ki - li - ze
27
S
Ba - ba tu - si - ki - li - ze tu - si - ki - li - ze Ba - ba tu - si - ki - li - ze
A
Ba - ba tu - si - ki - li - ze tu - si - ki - li - ze Ba - ba tu - si - ki - li - ze
T
Ba - ba tu - si - ki - li - e Ba - ba tu - si - ki - li - e
B
Ba - ba tu - si - ki - li - e Ba - ba tu - si - ki - li - e

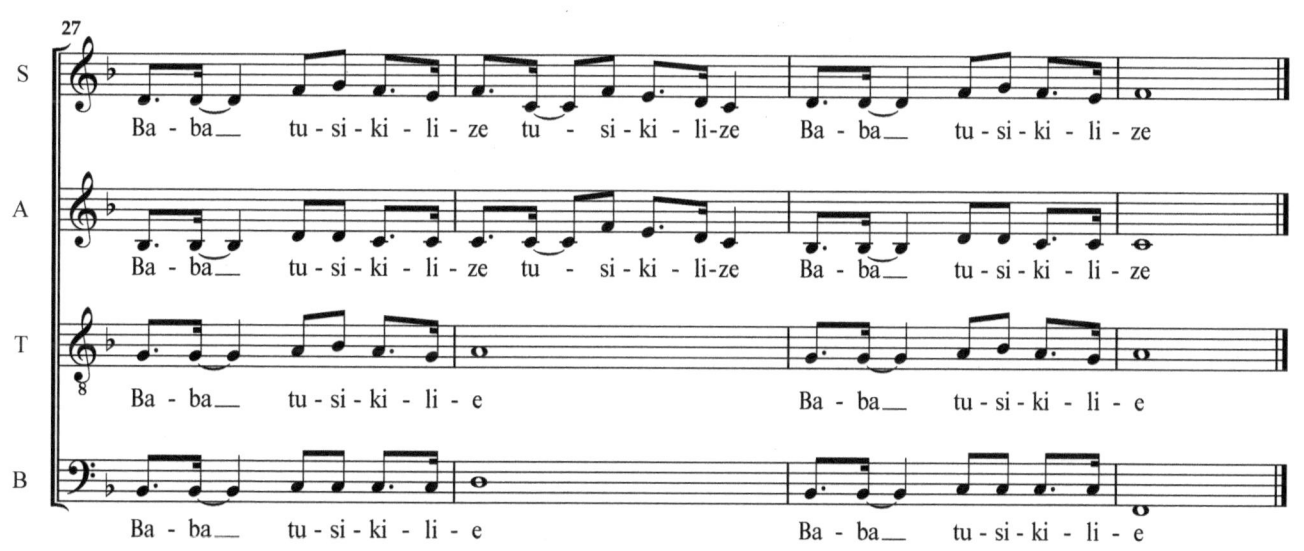

Ewe Mungu Baba Bariki
Offeratory Collection

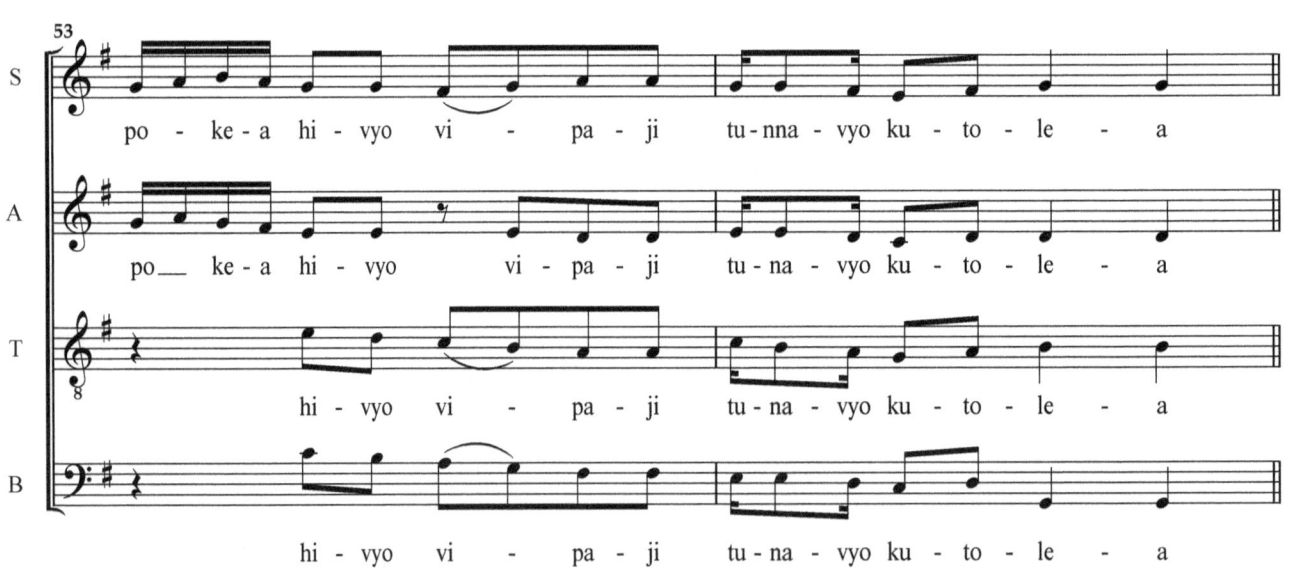

Mungu Tunaleta Sadaka
Offeratory Procession

Mungu Tunaleta Sadaka

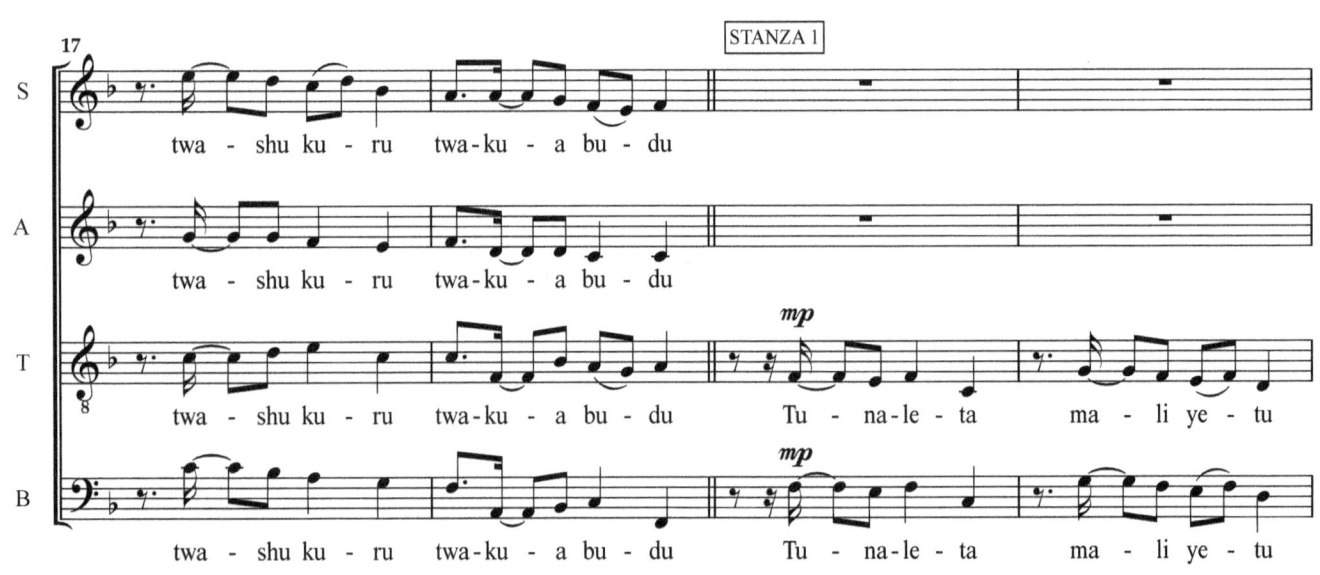

Mungu Tunaleta Sadaka

Mungu Tunaleta Sadaka

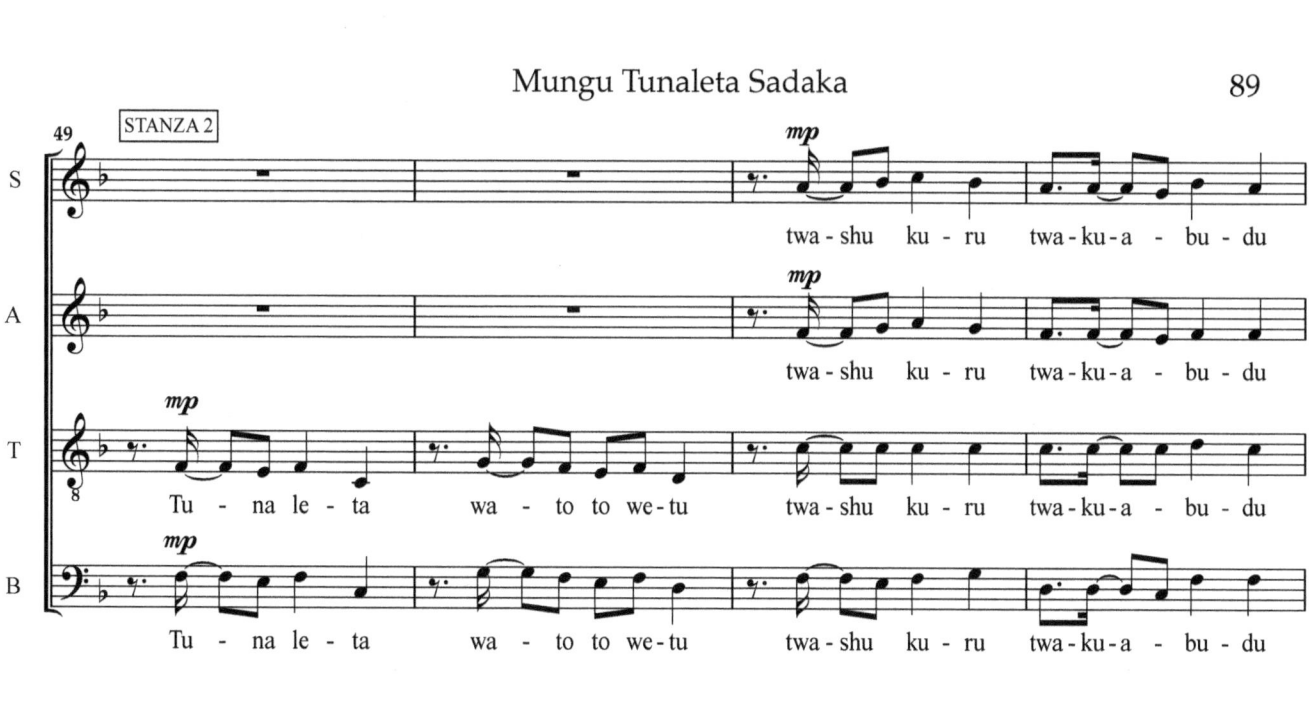
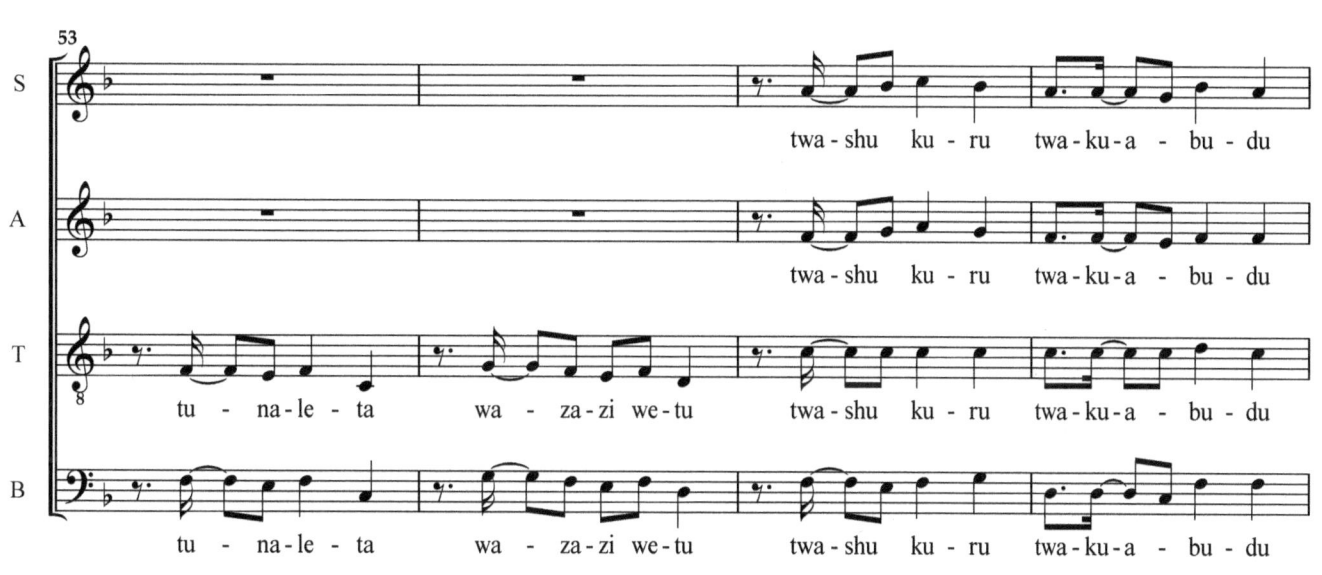

Mtakatifu
Sanctus

Kristu Alikufa, Kristu Alifufuka
Proclamation of the Mystery

Kristu Alikufa, Kristu Alifufuka

Pamoja Naye
Lesser Doxology

Amina
Amen

Baba Yetu
Pater Nostre

Baba Yetu

107

Baba Yetu

Amani ya Bwana
The Sign of Peace

Amani ya Bwana

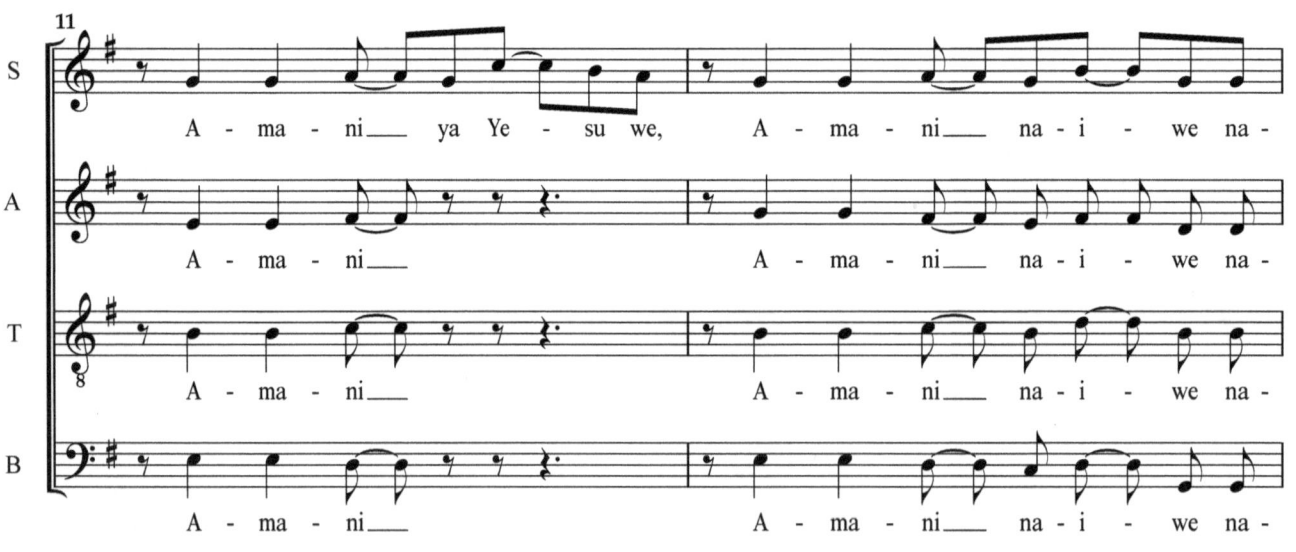

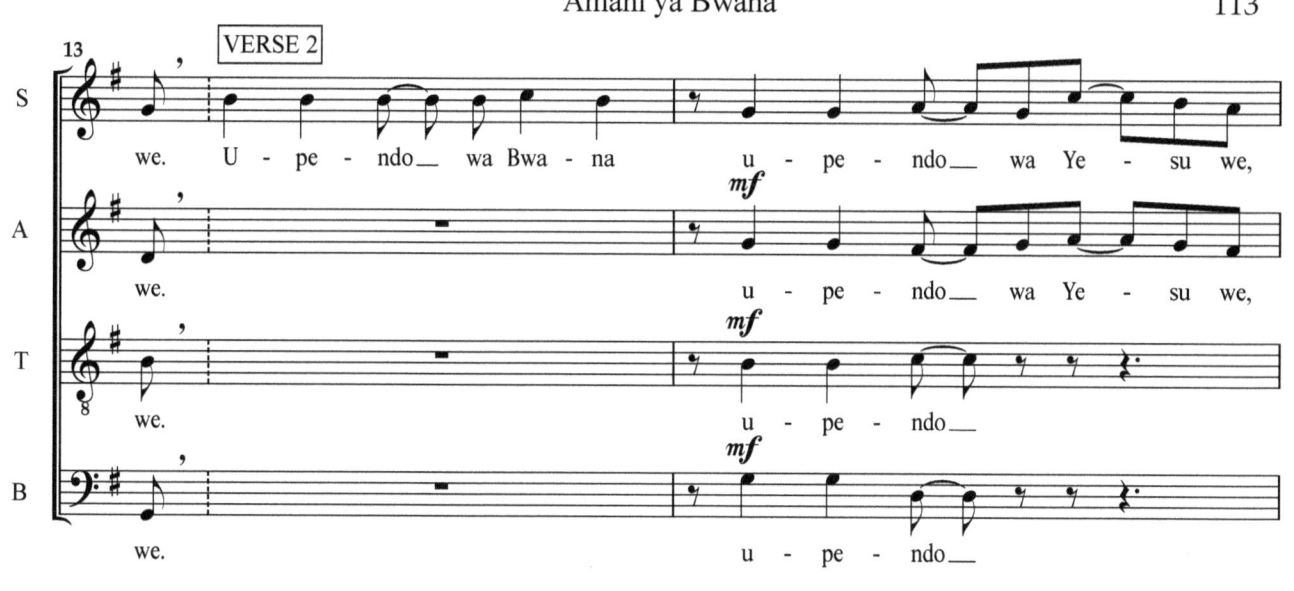

Amani ya Bwana

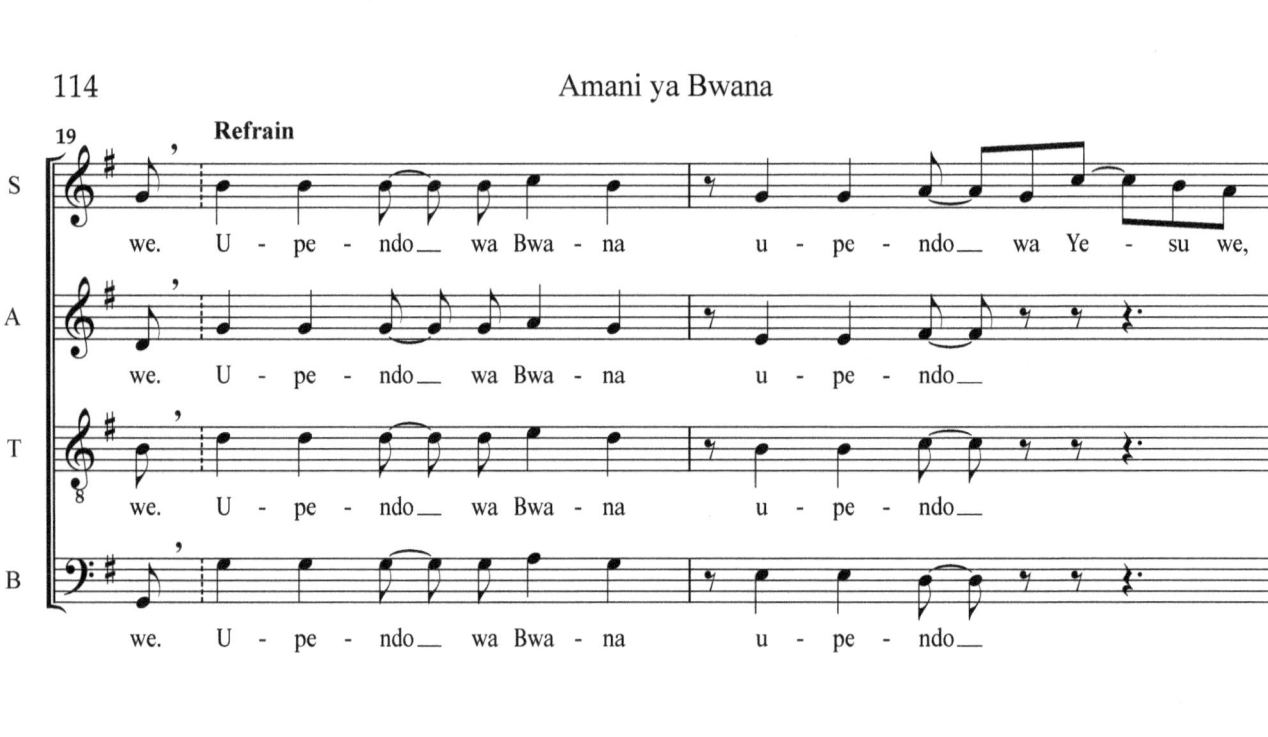

Amani ya Bwana

Amani ya Bwana

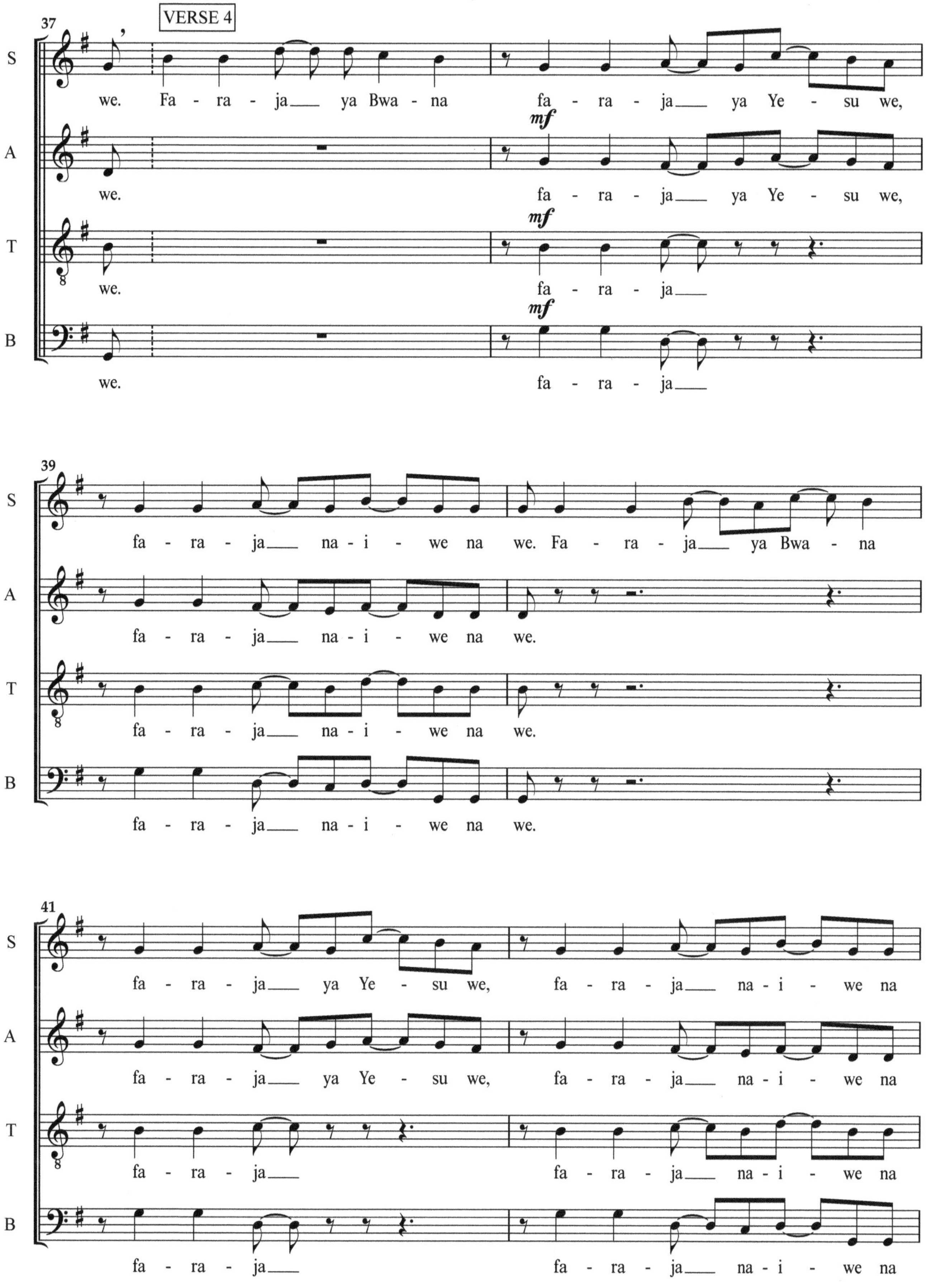
37
VERSE 4
S
A
T
B
mf
we. Fa - ra - ja ya Bwa - na fa - ra - ja ya Ye - su we,
we. fa - ra - ja ya Ye - su we,
we. fa - ra - ja
we. fa - ra - ja
39
fa - ra - ja na - i - we na we. Fa - ra - ja ya Bwa - na
fa - ra - ja na - i - we na we.
fa - ra - ja na - i - we na we.
fa - ra - ja na - i - we na we.
41
fa - ra - ja ya Ye - su we, fa - ra - ja na - i - we na
fa - ra - ja ya Ye - su we, fa - ra - ja na - i - we na
fa - ra - ja fa - ra - ja na - i - we na
fa - ra - ja fa - ra - ja na - i - we na

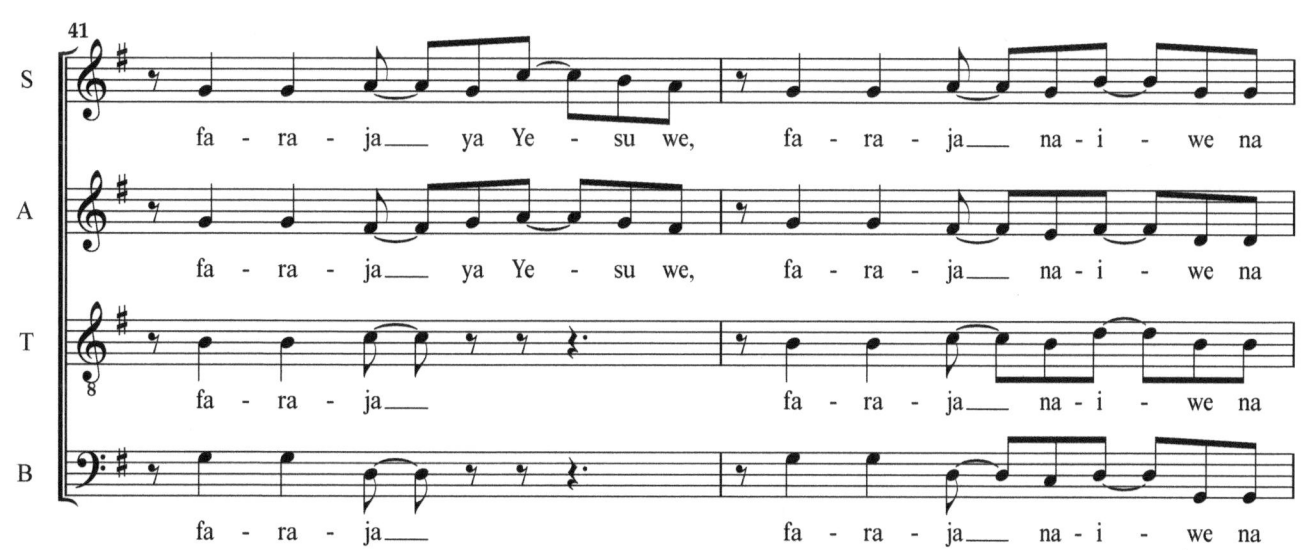

Amani ya Bwana

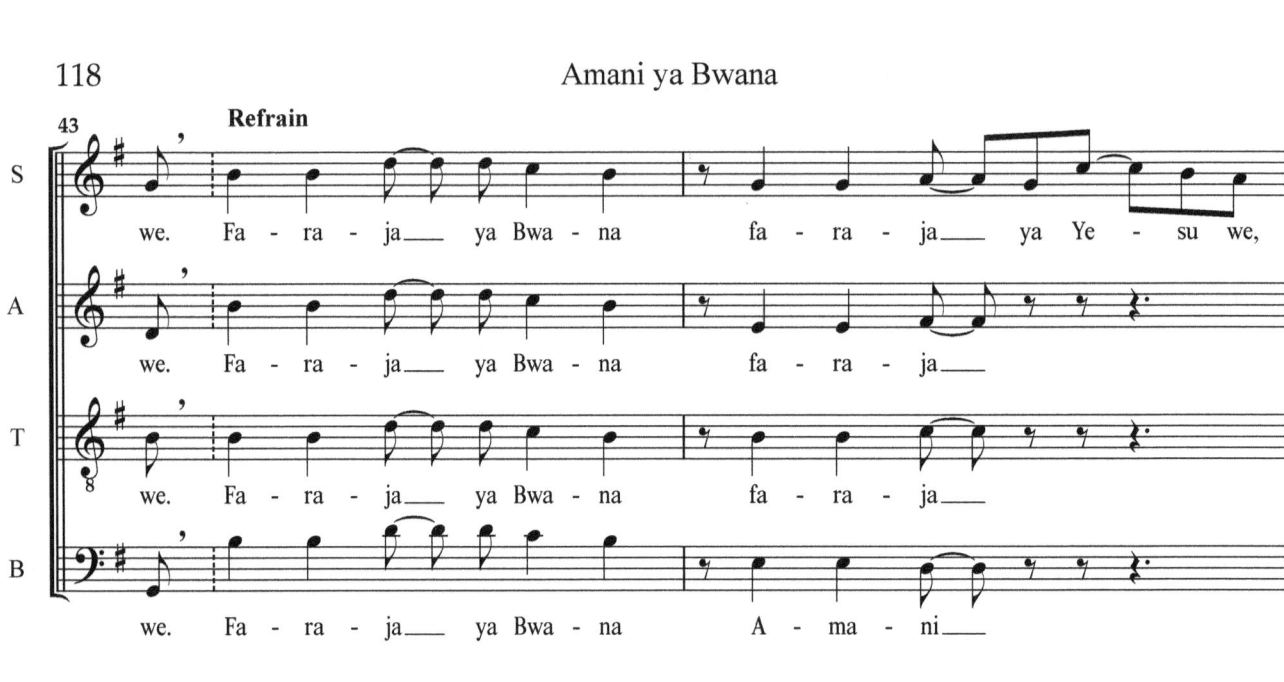

Amani ya Bwana

Ee Mwna Kondoo
Agnus Dei

Ee Mwna Kondoo

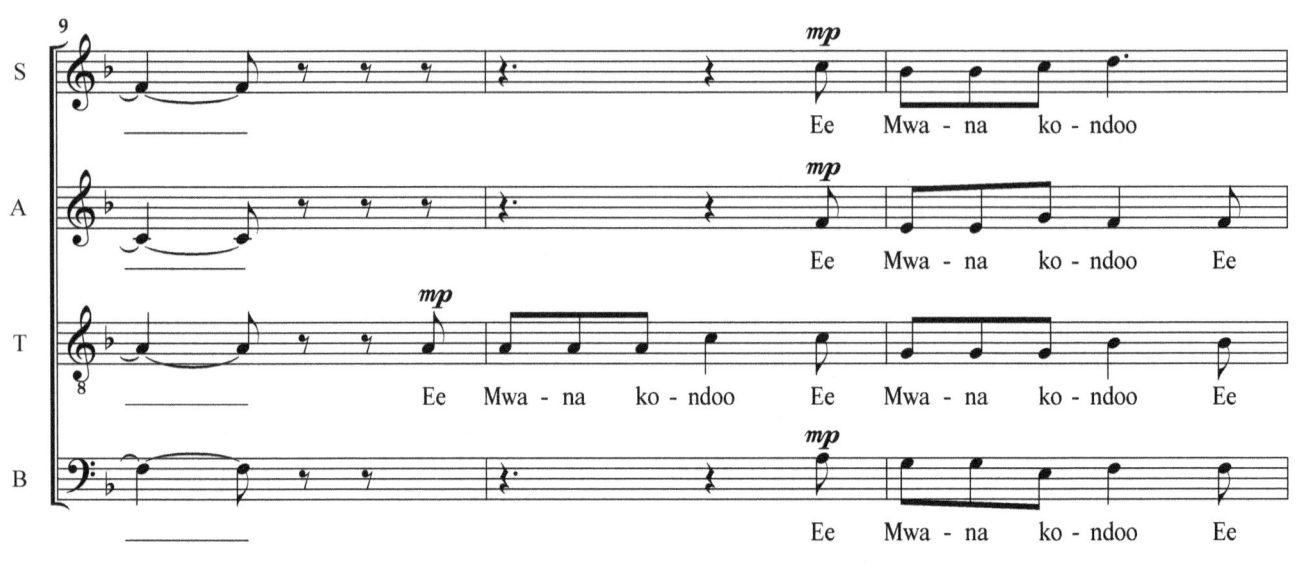

Ee Mwna Kondoo

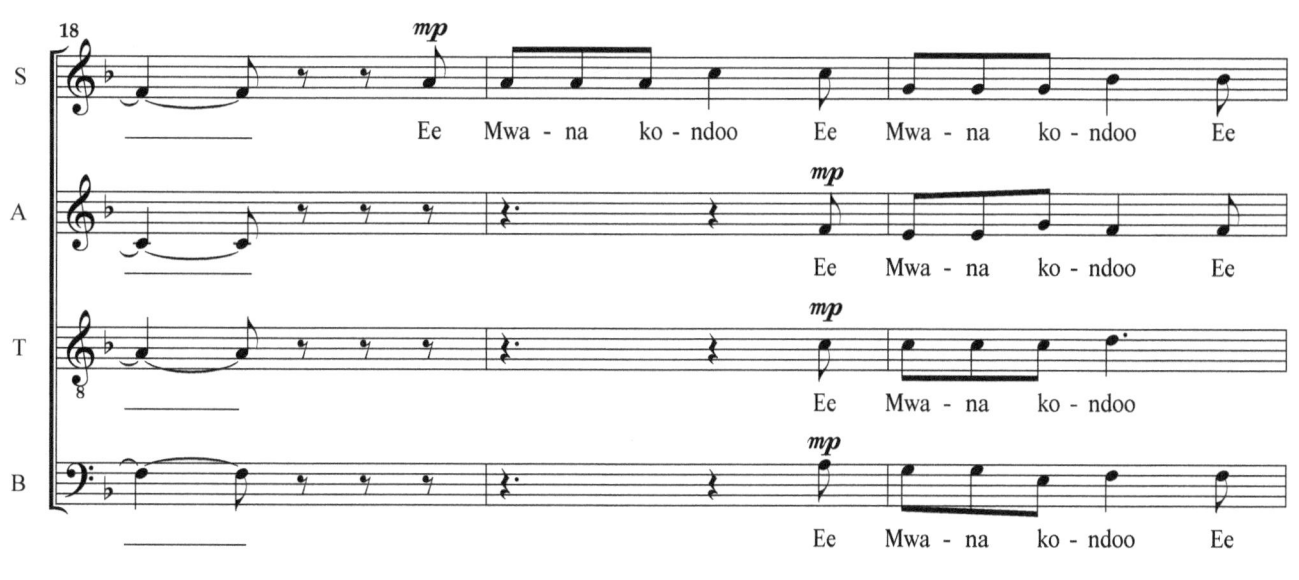

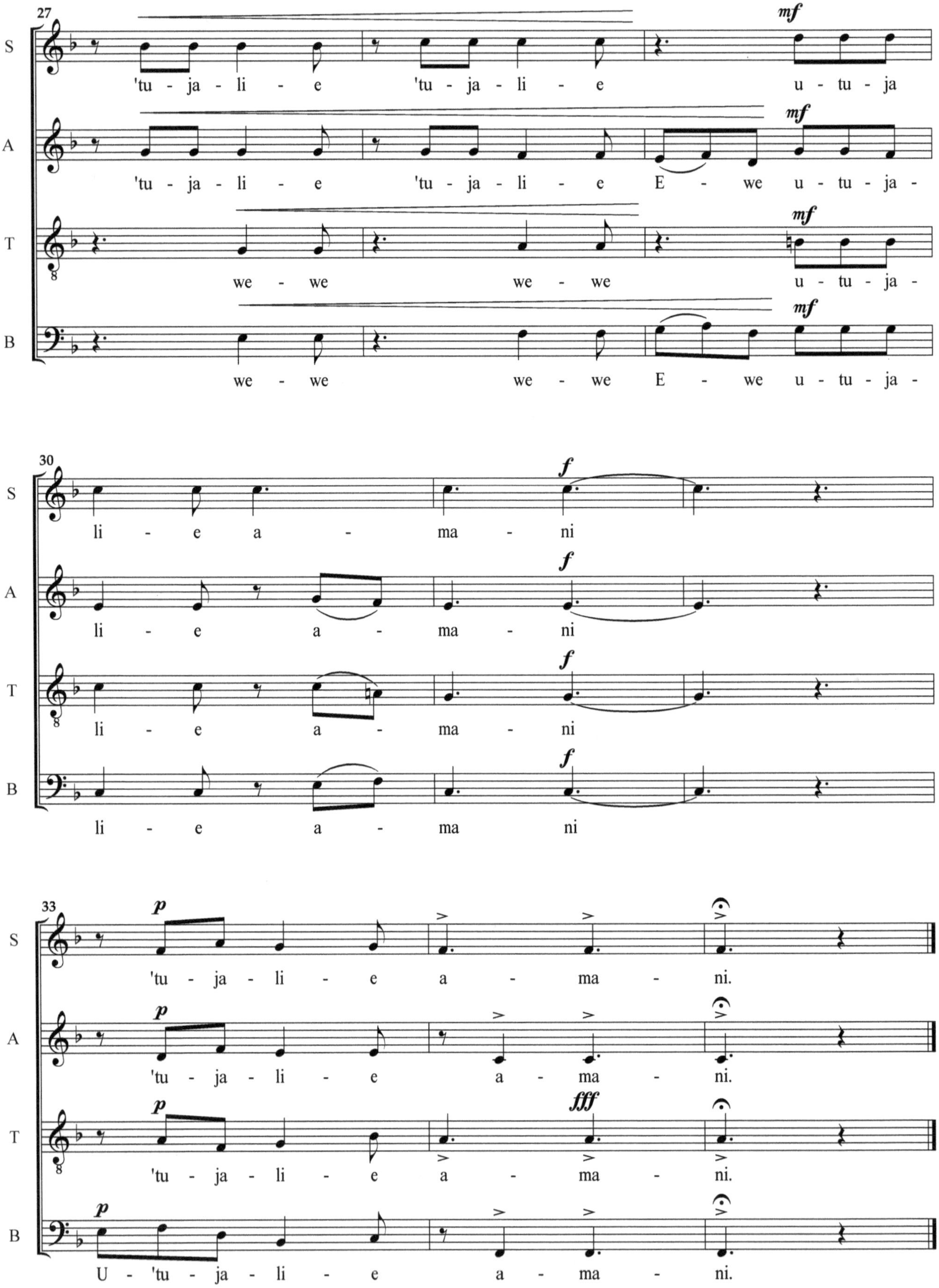
27
S
mf
'tu - ja - li - e 'tu - ja - li - e u - tu - ja
A
mf
'tu - ja - li - e 'tu - ja - li - e E - we u - tu - ja -
T
mf
we - we we - we u - tu - ja -
B
mf
we - we we - we E - we u - tu - ja -
30
S
f
li - e a - ma - ni
A
f
li - e a - ma - ni
T
f
li - e a - ma - ni
B
f
li - e a - ma ni
33
S
p
'tu - ja - li - e a - ma - ni.
A
p
'tu - ja - li - e a - ma - ni.
T
p
fff
'tu - ja - li - e a - ma - ni.
B
p
U - 'tu - ja - li - e a - ma - ni.

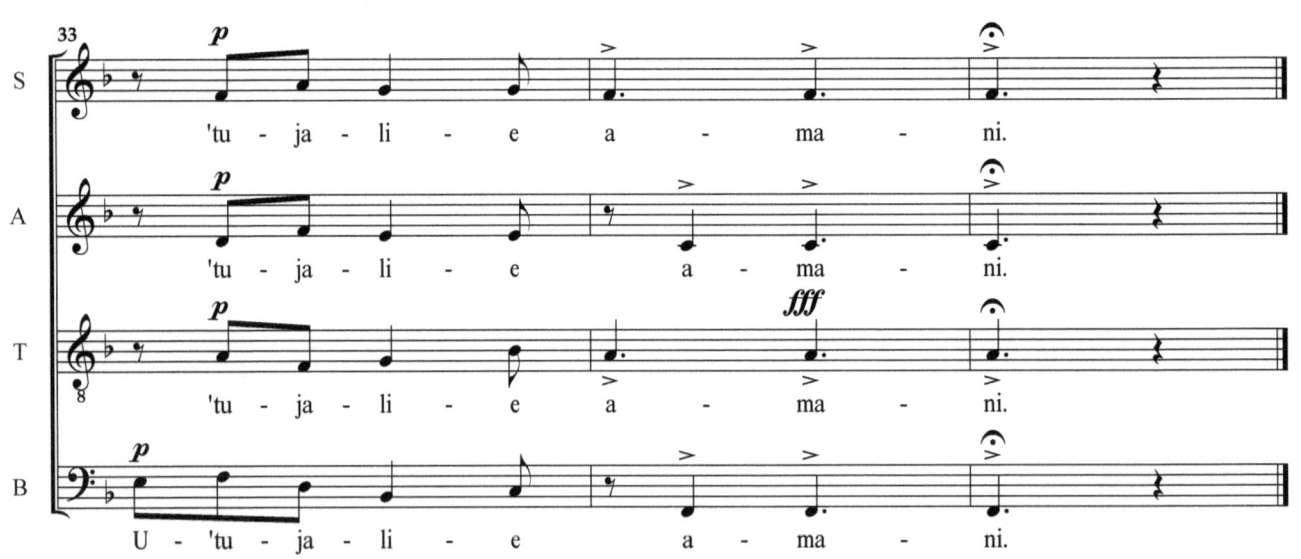

Posho la Mbinguni

Posho la Mbinguni

Posho la Mbinguini

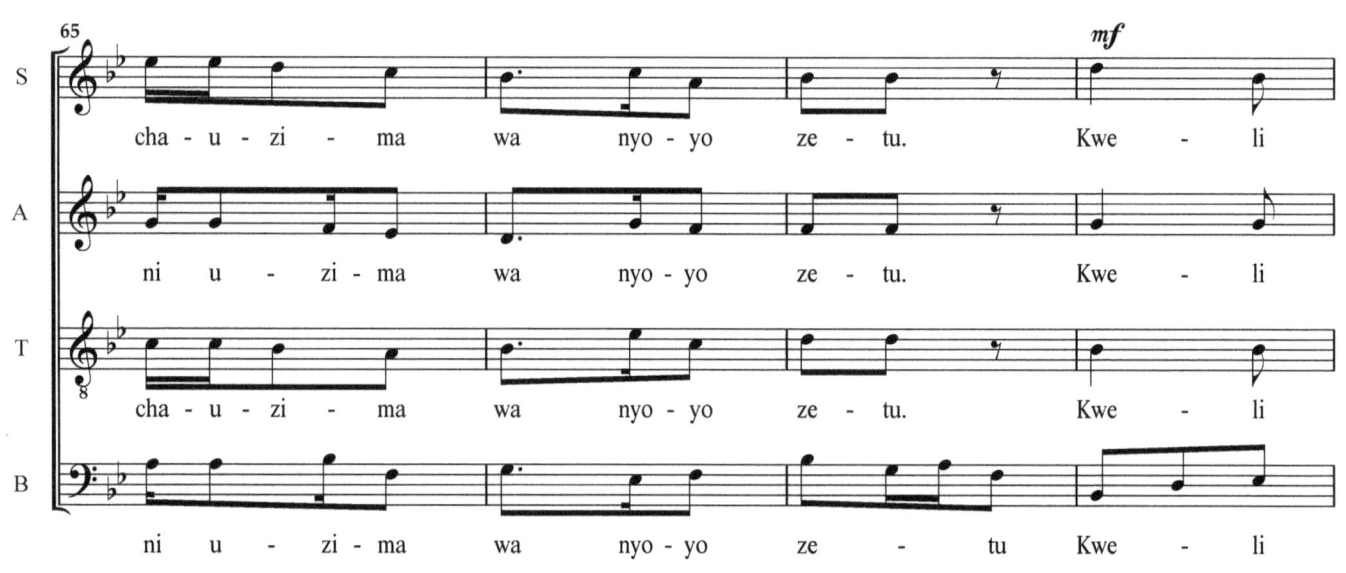

97
S
A
T
B
mp
wa ro - ho ze - tu We - we
wa ro - ho ze - tu.
wa ro - ho ze - tu.
wa ro - ho ze - tu. Bwa - na Ye - su we - we ndi - we
101
chem - che - mi ya mbi - ngu - ni, Bwa - na Ye - su da - mu ya - ko
We - we kwe - li Bwa - na Ye - su da - mu ya - ko
We - we Bwa - na Ye - su da - mu ya - ko
chem - che - mi ya mbi - ngu - ni kwe - li Bwa - na Ye - su da - mu ya - ko
105
ni ki - nywa - ji cha - u - zi - ma
cha - ku - la cha kwe - li te - na ni u - zi - ma
te - na ni ki - nywa - ji cha - u - zi - ma
ki - nywa - ji cha kwe - li te - na ni u - zi - ma

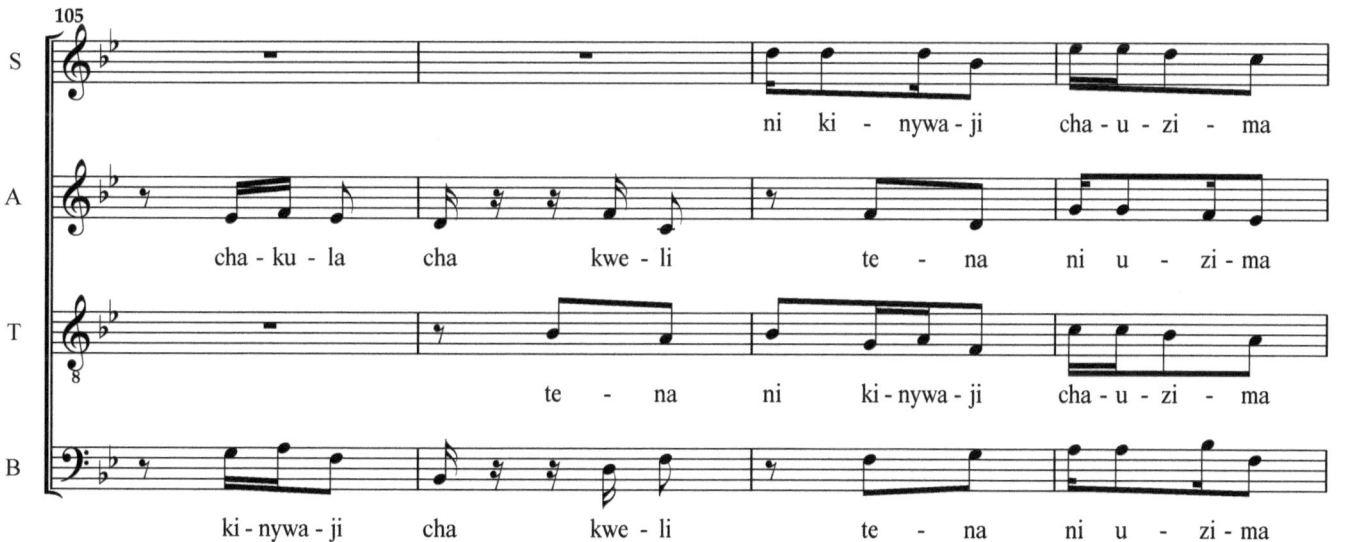

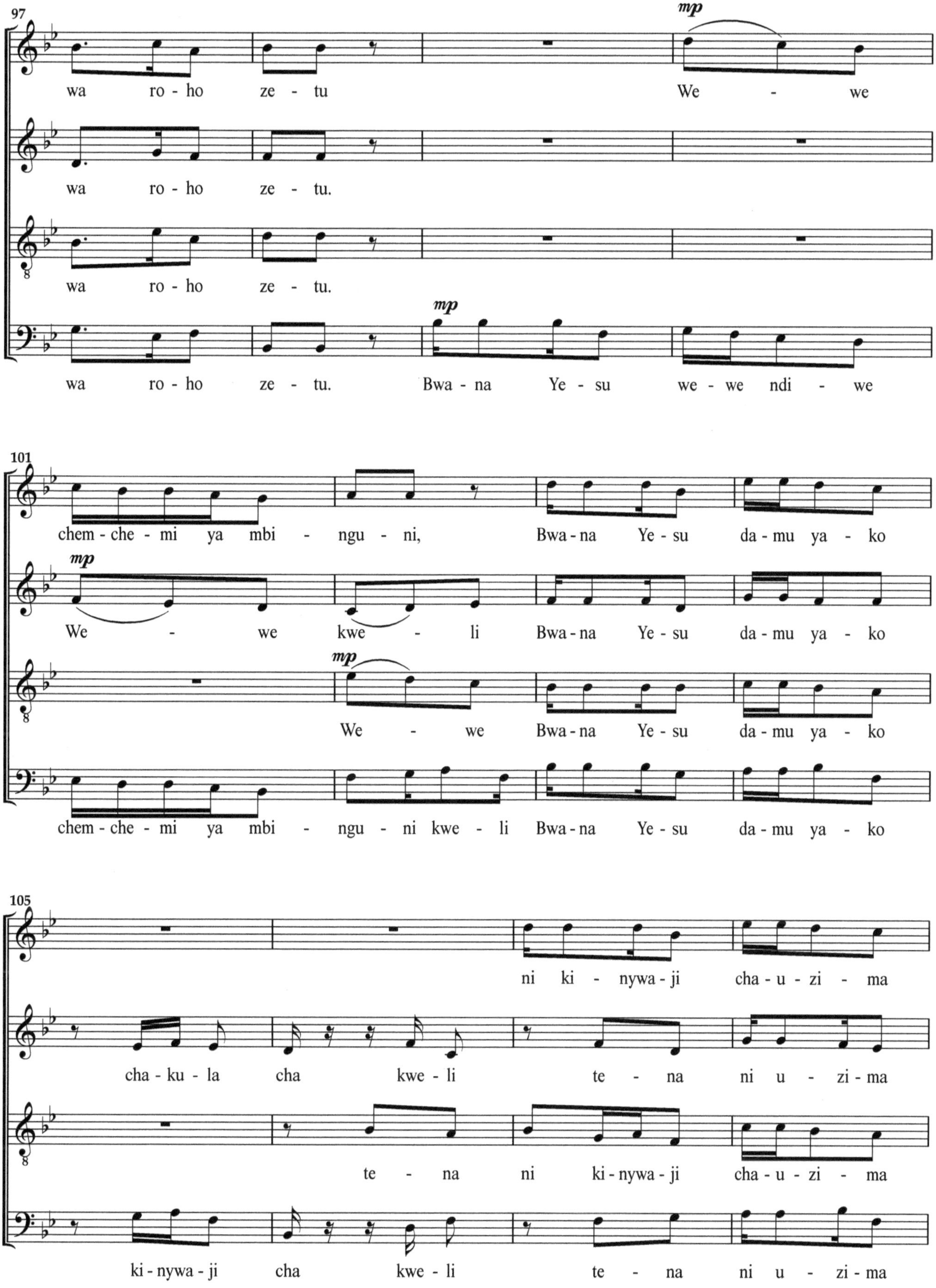

Posho la Mbinguini

Posho la Mbinguini

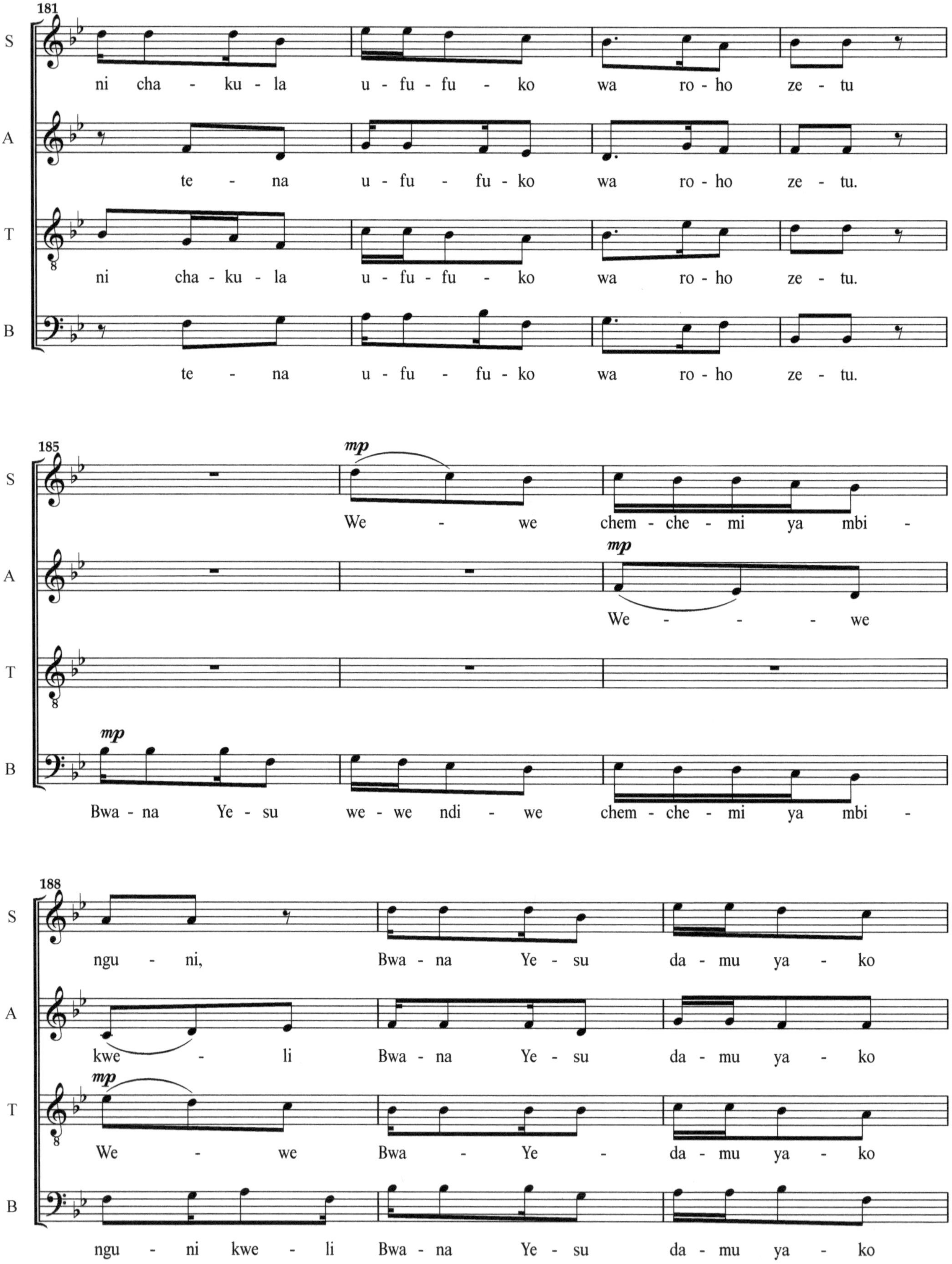
181
S
ni cha - ku - la u - fu - fu - ko wa ro - ho ze - tu
A
te - na u - fu - fu - ko wa ro - ho ze - tu.
T
ni cha - ku - la u - fu - fu - ko wa ro - ho ze - tu.
B
te - na u - fu - fu - ko wa ro - ho ze - tu.
185
S
mp
We - we chem - che - mi ya mbi -
A
mp
We - - - we
T
B
mp
Bwa - na Ye - su we - we ndi - we chem - che - mi ya mbi -
188
S
ngu - ni, Bwa - na Ye - su da - mu ya - ko
A
kwe - li Bwa - na Ye - su da - mu ya - ko
T
mp
We - we Bwa - Ye - da - mu ya - ko
B
ngu - ni kwe - li Bwa - na Ye - su da - mu ya - ko

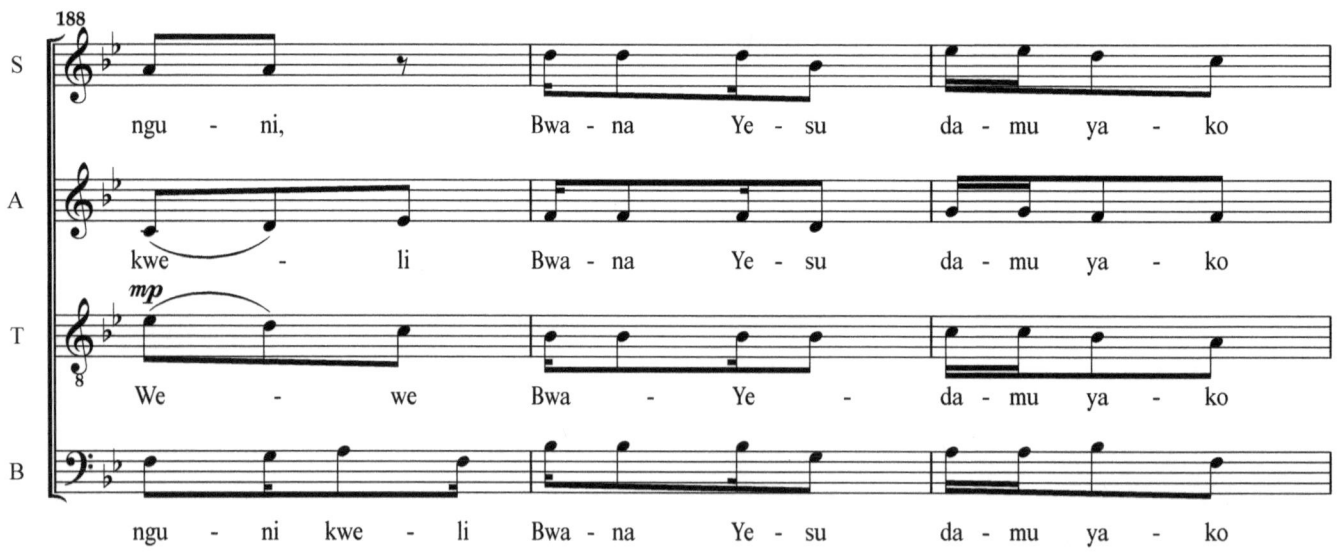

Posho la Mbinguini

142

Kusali Kweli ni Heria

Kusali Kweli ni Heri

Kusali Kweli ni Heri

Kusali Kweli ni Heri

145

49
S
A
T
B
p
Ku sa - li kwe - li kwe - li ni he - ri ku - sa - li - kwe - li
Ku - sa - li kwe - li kwe - li ni he - ri kwe - li
we - we tu kwe - li kwe - li ni he - ri kwe - li
we - we tu kwe - li kwe - li ni he - ri kwe - li
53
cresc.
mf
kwe - li ni he - ri fa - mi - li - a ye - nye ku - sa - li pa - mo - ja kwe - li pa -
kwe - li ni he - ri fa - mi - li - a ku - sa - li pa - mo - ja kwe - li pa -
kwe - li ni he - ri fa - mi - li - a ye - nye ku - sa - li pa - mo - ja kwe - li pa -
kwe - li ni he - ri fa - mi li - a ku - sa - li pa - mo - ja kwe - li pa -
57
mo - ja 'ta - ka - vyo i - shi kwe - li pa - mo ja 'ta - ka - vyo - i - shi
mo - ja 'ta - ka - vyo i - shi kwe - li 'ta - ka - vyo i - shi
mo - ja 'ta - ka - vyo - i - shi kwe - li pa - mo - ja 'ta - ka - vyo - i - shi
mo - ja 'ta - ka - vyo - i - shi kwe - li 'ta - ka - vyo - i - shi

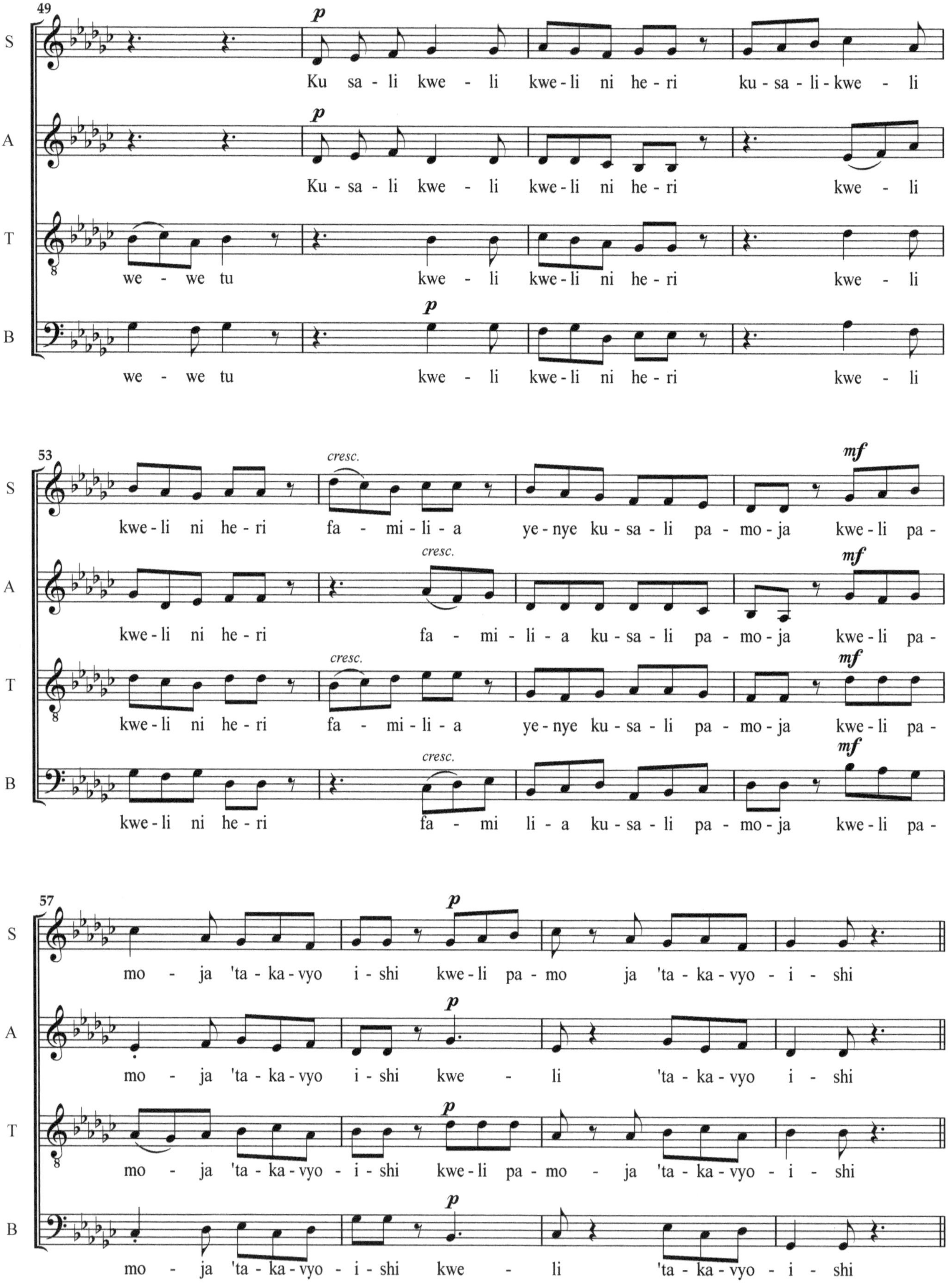

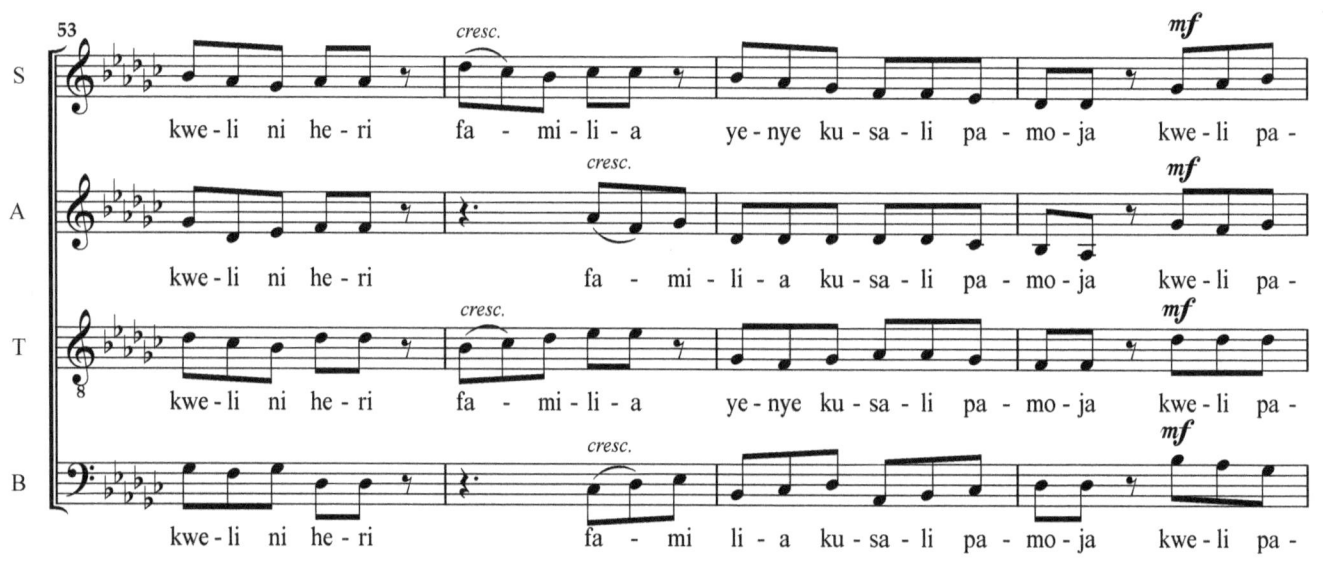

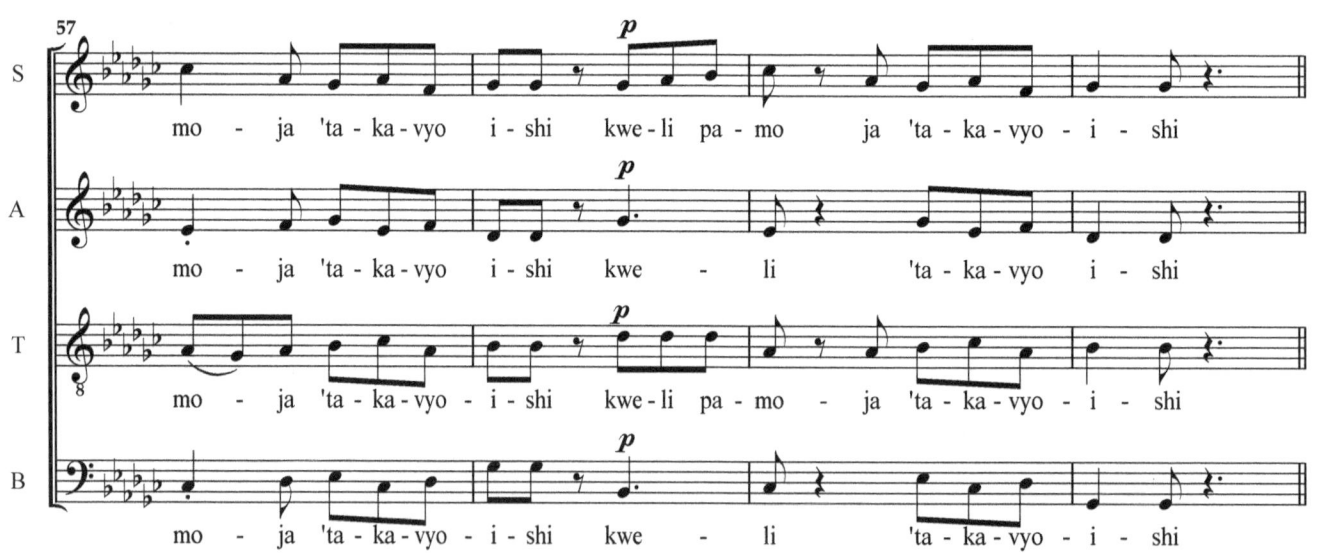

Kusali Kweli ni Heri

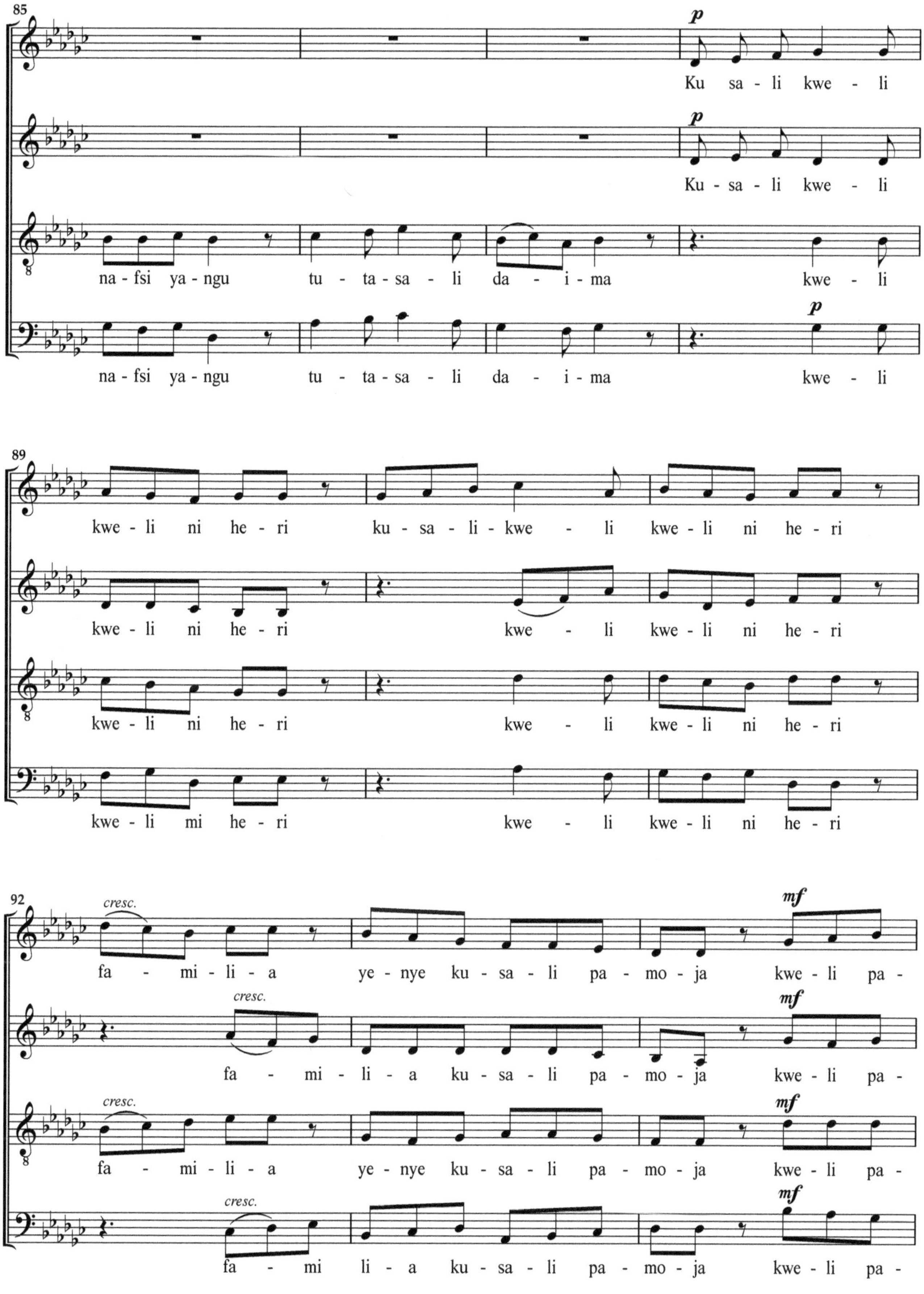
85
S
A
T
B
p
Ku sa - li kwe - li
p
Ku - sa - li kwe - li
na - fsi ya - ngu tu - ta - sa - li da - i - ma kwe - li
p
na - fsi ya - ngu tu - ta - sa - li da - i - ma kwe - li
89
kwe - li ni he - ri ku - sa - li - kwe - li kwe - li ni he - ri
kwe - li ni he - ri kwe - li kwe - li ni he - ri
kwe - li ni he - ri kwe - li kwe - li ni he - ri
kwe - li mi he - ri kwe - li kwe - li ni he - ri
92
cresc.
mf
fa - mi - li - a ye - nye ku - sa - li pa - mo - ja kwe - li pa -
cresc.
mf
fa - mi - li - a ku - sa - li pa - mo - ja kwe - li pa -
cresc.
mf
fa - mi - li - a ye - nye ku - sa - li pa - mo - ja kwe - li pa -
cresc.
mf
fa - mi li - a ku - sa - li pa - mo - ja kwe - li pa -

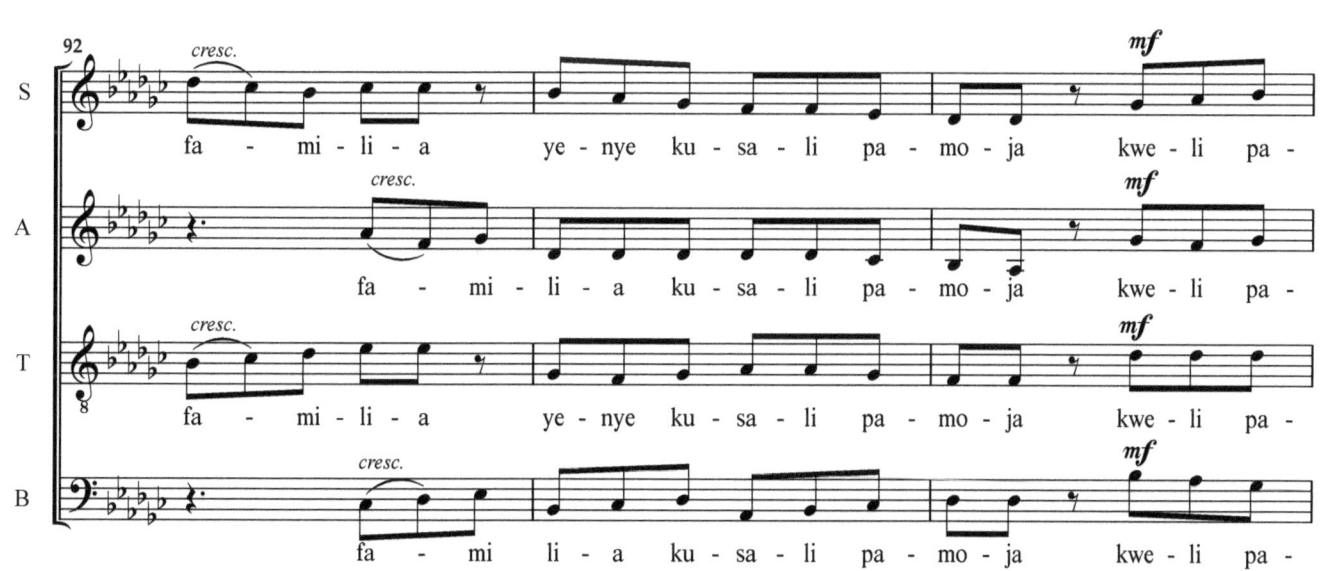

Nakutegemea Mwenyezi

Nakutegemea Mwenyezi

Nakutegemea Mwenyezi

Nakutegemea Mwenyezi

Nakutegemea Mwenyezi

Nakutegemea Mwenyezi

Nakutegemea Mwenyezi

Nakutegemea Mwenyezi

Nakutegemea Mwenyezi

Nakutegemea Mwenyezi

Nakutegemea Mwenyezi

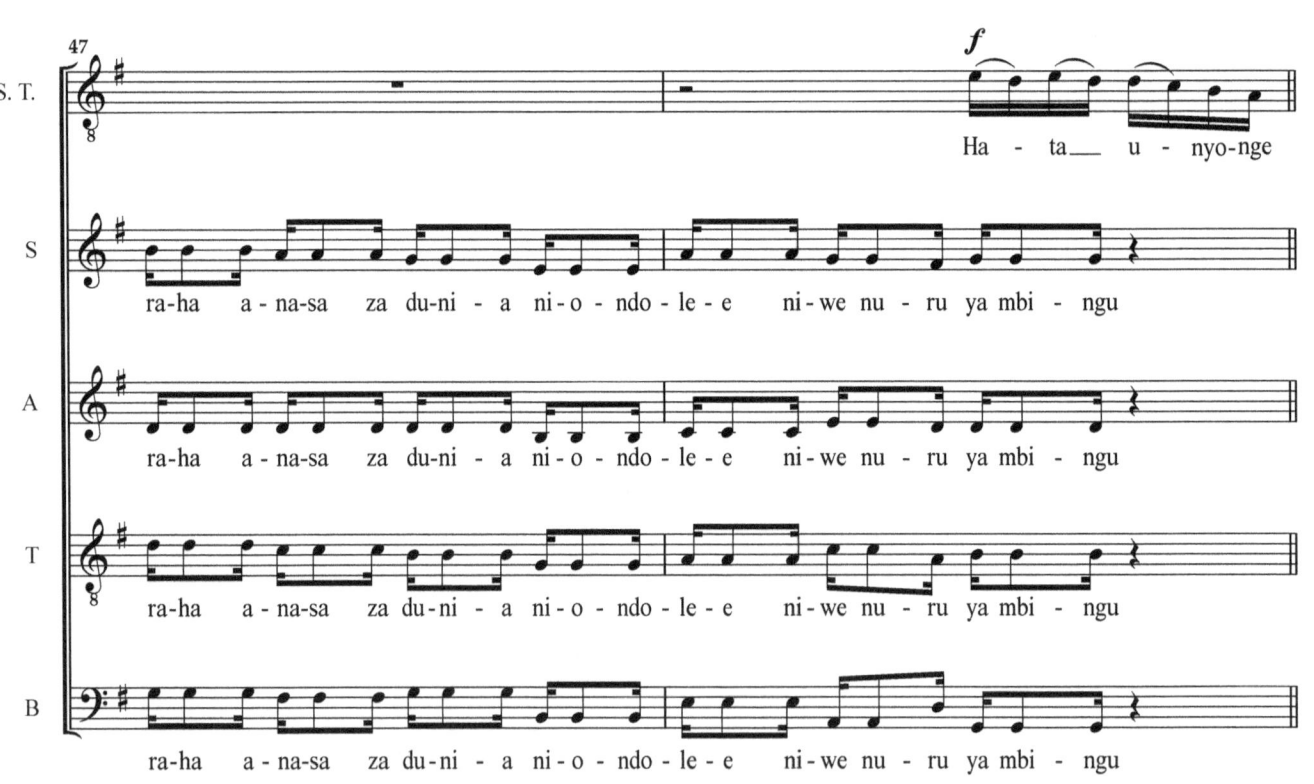

Nakutegemea Mwenyezi

163

Nakutegemea Mwenyezi

Nakutegemea Mwenyezi

Nakutegemea Mwenyezi

Nakutegemea Mwenyezi

Nakutegemea Mwenyezi

Nakutegemea Mwenyezi

Unirehemu Unitakase
Recessional Hymn

Unirehemu Unitakase

Unirehemu Unitakase

www.ingramcontent.com/pod-product-compliance
Lightning Source LLC
Chambersburg PA
CBHW040000080526
44586CB00027B/2825